Advanced SBA Commercial Mortgage Loan Structuring

How to Structure Complex SBA Mortgage Deals and Maximize Approval Chances

By Joseph G. Correa

Licensed Mortgage Broker, Finibi Mortgage

Copyright & Legal Notice

Published by Live Stronger Faster

The information provided in this book is for educational and informational purposes only and does not constitute financial, legal, tax, or investment advice. Although the author is a licensed mortgage professional, the content presented is general in nature and is not intended as personalized guidance for any specific individual, business, or financial situation.

The strategies, loan structures, and examples discussed in this book are illustrative and educational in nature. They are intended to demonstrate concepts related to SBA commercial mortgage financing, including SBA 7(a) and 504 loan programs, borrower qualification, debt service coverage analysis, property acquisition, refinancing, construction financing, and advanced loan structuring. These examples do not represent guaranteed approvals, loan terms, or outcomes. Results may vary significantly based on individual financial profiles, credit history, business performance, property type, market conditions, and lender-specific guidelines.

SBA loan programs are subject to eligibility requirements, regulatory guidelines, and changes established by the U.S. Small Business Administration and participating lenders. Borrowers are encouraged to consult directly with qualified financial, legal, and tax professionals before making any financing or investment decisions.

The author and publisher make no representations or warranties regarding the accuracy, completeness, or applicability of the content and disclaim any liability for errors, omissions, or outcomes resulting from the use or misuse of the information contained in this book.

First Edition, 2026

Table of Contents

Introduction

In the world of commercial real estate and business financing, the difference between a denied loan and a fully approved, cash-flowing deal often comes down to one critical skill: structuring. While many borrowers and even loan professionals focus heavily on credit scores, income, or collateral, seasoned investors and top-performing loan originators understand that the real power lies in how a deal is put together. Structuring is not just about meeting guidelines—it is about strategically aligning every component of a transaction to fit within SBA requirements while maximizing flexibility, profitability, and long-term growth. This book represents the culmination of everything covered in this series and takes you into the advanced strategies that separate average deals from elite ones.

By the time you reach this point in the SBA Commercial Mortgage Loan Mastery Series, you already understand the fundamentals, approval strategies, property types, and loan programs such as SBA 7(a) and 504 loans. You have explored how to acquire owner-occupied properties, refinance debt, and even use SBA financing for construction and expansion. Now, the focus shifts to mastery. This is where you begin to think like a deal architect rather than just a borrower or broker. You will learn how to structure transactions in a way that solves problems, overcomes obstacles, and creates opportunities where others see limitations.

Advanced structuring begins with a mindset shift. Instead of asking, "Will this deal get approved?" you start asking, "How can I structure this deal so it gets approved?" This subtle difference changes everything. It forces you to think creatively within the framework of SBA guidelines, to understand lender overlays, and to identify multiple paths to approval. Every deal has variables—borrower profile, business financials, property type, loan purpose, and risk factors. The key is knowing how to adjust those variables strategically.

One of the most important concepts you will learn in this book is that there is rarely just one way to structure a deal. A transaction that appears weak at first glance can often be repositioned into a strong, approvable file with the right adjustments. This could involve restructuring ownership percentages, adjusting the use of proceeds, reallocating debt, introducing additional collateral, or leveraging multiple businesses within a single loan structure. The SBA framework is more flexible than most people realize, and those who understand how to navigate it gain a significant competitive advantage. Another major focus of advanced structuring is risk mitigation. Lenders are not simply approving loans—they are evaluating risk. Your ability to structure a deal in a way that reduces perceived risk is what increases your chances of approval. This may involve strengthening the borrower's profile through compensating factors, improving cash flow coverage, or presenting a clear and compelling narrative that explains the business's stability and growth potential. A well-structured deal tells a story that makes sense to underwriters, credit committees, and lenders.

Cash flow is at the center of every SBA loan decision, and advanced structuring often revolves around optimizing how income and expenses are presented. This includes understanding how to normalize financials, add back legitimate expenses, and position the business in the strongest possible light. It also involves analyzing debt service coverage ratios and ensuring that the deal meets or exceeds lender expectations. In many cases, structuring can make the difference between a marginal file and a strong approval by simply presenting the financials more effectively.

In addition to financial structuring, you will also explore ownership and entity structuring. SBA loans often involve multiple parties, operating companies, and real estate holding entities. Knowing how to properly structure these relationships is critical. This includes understanding eligibility requirements, affiliation rules, and how to align ownership structures with SBA guidelines. When done correctly, entity structuring can enhance flexibility, protect assets, and improve overall deal viability.

Collateral is another powerful tool in advanced structuring. While SBA loans are primarily cash flow-driven, collateral still plays an important role in strengthening a deal. You will learn how to use additional collateral strategically, when it is necessary, and how it can compensate for other weaknesses in a file. This includes real estate, business assets, and even personal assets when appropriate. The goal is not just to add collateral, but to use it intelligently to support the overall structure of the transaction.

Loan purpose and use of proceeds also become increasingly important at the advanced level. SBA loans can be used for a wide range of purposes, including acquisitions, refinancing, construction, equipment purchases, and working capital. However, how these funds are allocated within a deal can significantly impact approval. Structuring the use of proceeds correctly ensures compliance with SBA guidelines while maximizing the benefit to the borrower. This requires a deep understanding of program rules and lender preferences.

As you progress through this book, you will also learn how to handle complex scenarios that often challenge borrowers and loan professionals. These may include mixed-use properties, partial ownership buyouts, partner buy-ins, business acquisitions with real estate components, and deals involving multiple revenue streams. These are the types of transactions that require advanced structuring techniques and a thorough understanding of SBA guidelines. Mastering these scenarios opens the door to larger and more profitable opportunities.

Another key element of advanced structuring is understanding lender behavior. Not all lenders interpret SBA guidelines the same way. Each lender has its own overlays, risk tolerance, and preferred deal types. Knowing how to match a deal with the right lender is just as important as structuring the deal itself. This book will help you understand how to position your transaction for the best possible lender fit, increasing both efficiency and approval likelihood.

You will also gain insight into how to present a deal effectively. Even the best-structured transaction can fail if it is not communicated clearly. This includes organizing documentation, presenting financials, and creating a narrative that highlights the strengths of the deal. Underwriters and credit committees rely on the information you provide, and your ability to present that information professionally can make a significant difference in the outcome. Advanced structuring is not just about getting deals approved—it is about building a scalable strategy for long-term success. Whether you are a borrower looking to grow your business portfolio or a loan professional aiming to close more deals, the skills you develop in this book will allow you to operate at a higher level. You will be able to identify opportunities others miss, solve problems more effectively, and create financing solutions that drive growth.

Throughout this book, you will notice that many of the strategies are interconnected. Structuring is not a single step—it is a comprehensive process that involves analyzing every aspect of a deal and aligning it with SBA requirements and lender expectations. It requires attention to detail, creativity, and a deep understanding of how all the pieces fit together. The more you practice these concepts, the more intuitive they will become.

It is also important to recognize that advanced structuring requires continuous learning. SBA guidelines evolve, lender preferences change, and market conditions shift. Staying informed and adaptable is essential. This book provides a strong foundation, but your success will depend on your ability to apply these principles in real-world scenarios and continue refining your approach over time.

As you move forward, remember that every complex deal represents an opportunity. While others may walk away from challenging transactions, you now have the tools to approach them with confidence. Instead of seeing obstacles, you will begin to see possibilities. This mindset is what separates top performers from the rest of the market.

This final book in the series is designed to elevate your understanding and give you the confidence to handle even the most sophisticated SBA commercial mortgage transactions. It brings together everything you have learned and pushes you into the realm of true expertise. By mastering advanced structuring, you position yourself not only to succeed but to lead in the world of SBA financing.

The journey from beginner to expert is not defined by how many deals you see, but by how well you understand them. With the knowledge and strategies presented in this book, you are now equipped to structure deals at a professional level, maximize approval chances, and build a powerful foundation for long-term growth in commercial real estate and business financing.

Chapter 1

The Architecture of Advanced SBA Commercial Mortgage Loan Structuring

At the highest level of SBA commercial mortgage lending, structuring is no longer a basic process of filling out an application and submitting documents. It becomes an art and a science combined—a disciplined approach to assembling a deal in a way that aligns borrower goals, SBA guidelines, lender expectations, and risk management principles into one cohesive and approvable transaction. This chapter introduces you to the architecture of advanced deal structuring, where every component of a loan is intentionally designed to work together. Instead of reacting to problems after submission, you begin structuring deals proactively from the very beginning.

The foundation of advanced structuring starts with understanding that every SBA loan is evaluated through multiple lenses simultaneously. These include borrower strength, business performance, property quality, cash flow stability, and overall risk. Each of these components can either strengthen or weaken a deal depending on how it is presented and aligned. The goal is not to have a perfect deal in every category, but rather to create a balanced structure where strengths compensate for weaknesses. This concept is known as layering compensating factors, and it is one of the most powerful tools in advanced structuring.

A key principle in structuring is control over variables. Every deal contains variables that can be adjusted, including loan amount, down payment, ownership structure, business income presentation, and use of proceeds. Many borrowers and inexperienced loan professionals treat these variables as fixed, but in reality, they are flexible within the boundaries of SBA guidelines. Advanced structuring involves identifying which variables can be adjusted and how those adjustments can improve the overall strength of the deal. For example, increasing a down payment may improve lender confidence, while restructuring ownership percentages may help meet eligibility requirements.

Cash flow remains the central pillar of SBA lending, and structuring revolves heavily around how cash flow is calculated, presented, and supported. This includes not only the business's historical income but also projected income and how it aligns with the loan's debt service requirements. Advanced structuring requires a deep understanding of how lenders analyze financial statements, including tax returns, profit and loss statements, and balance sheets. It also involves knowing how to normalize financials by adding back legitimate expenses such as depreciation, one-time costs, and discretionary expenses. These adjustments can significantly impact the debt service coverage ratio, which is one of the most critical approval metrics.

Another essential element of structuring is understanding the relationship between the operating business and the real estate. In many SBA transactions, especially those involving owner-occupied properties, the business and the property are closely tied together. Structuring these relationships correctly is crucial. This often involves creating or utilizing separate legal entities, such as an operating company and a real estate holding company, and ensuring that lease agreements between them meet SBA requirements. When done correctly, this structure can provide both operational flexibility and asset protection while still maintaining compliance.

Ownership structure plays a critical role in determining eligibility and approval. The SBA has specific rules regarding ownership percentages, affiliations, and guarantor requirements. Advanced structuring involves strategically organizing ownership in a way that meets these rules while also aligning with the goals of the borrowers. This may include adjusting ownership stakes to ensure that key individuals qualify as eligible borrowers or structuring partnerships in a way that strengthens the overall application. Understanding how ownership impacts both eligibility and risk is essential for successful deal structuring. Risk perception is another major factor that structuring seeks to influence. Lenders are constantly evaluating risk, and their decisions are based not only on numbers but also on how those numbers are interpreted. A well-structured deal reduces perceived risk by presenting a clear and logical narrative. This narrative explains how the business operates, how it generates income, and why it is likely to succeed in the future. Advanced structuring involves crafting this narrative in a way that addresses potential concerns before they become objections. This proactive approach can significantly increase approval chances.

Collateral, while secondary to cash flow in SBA lending, still plays an important role in structuring. Advanced structuring involves understanding when and how to use additional collateral to strengthen a deal. This could include pledging additional real estate, business assets, or even personal assets when necessary. The goal is not to rely solely on collateral but to use it as a strategic tool to support the overall structure of the deal. Properly used, collateral can provide lenders with additional confidence and help offset other perceived risks.

The use of proceeds is another area where structuring can have a significant impact. SBA loans allow for a variety of uses, including purchasing real estate, acquiring a business, refinancing debt, and funding construction or improvements. However, how these funds are allocated within a transaction must align with SBA guidelines. Advanced structuring involves carefully planning the use of proceeds to ensure compliance while maximizing the benefit to the borrower. This may include combining multiple uses into a single loan or structuring funds in a way that supports both immediate needs and long-term growth.

Lender selection is often overlooked but is a critical component of advanced structuring. Different lenders have different appetites for risk, preferences for certain types of deals, and interpretations of SBA guidelines. A deal that is declined by one lender may be approved by another simply because of these differences. Advanced structuring involves not only building a strong deal but also matching that deal with the right lender. This requires knowledge of the lending landscape and an understanding of which lenders are best suited for specific types of transactions.

Timing is another factor that plays a role in structuring. The timing of a transaction can impact everything from financial performance to market conditions. Advanced structuring involves considering when to move forward with a deal and how timing can be used strategically. For example, waiting for stronger financials or improved market conditions may enhance approval chances. Conversely, acting quickly in a favorable market may provide opportunities that would otherwise be missed.

Documentation and presentation are the final pieces of the structuring process. Even the best-structured deal can fail if it is not presented clearly and professionally. This includes organizing financial statements, preparing detailed explanations, and ensuring that all required documentation is complete and accurate. Advanced structuring involves thinking from the perspective of the underwriter and making it as easy as possible for them to understand and approve the deal. Clear and concise presentation reduces confusion and builds confidence.

As you develop your structuring skills, you will begin to see patterns and opportunities that others overlook. Deals that initially appear weak may reveal hidden strengths, while strong deals may require adjustments to reach their full potential. This ability to analyze and adapt is what defines advanced structuring. It allows you to approach each transaction with confidence and creativity, knowing that there are multiple paths to success.

Ultimately, advanced SBA commercial mortgage loan structuring is about control. It is about taking control of the variables, the narrative, and the overall direction of a deal. Instead of being limited by guidelines, you learn to work within them strategically. This shift in perspective transforms the way you approach lending and opens the door to more complex and profitable opportunities.

As you move through the rest of this book, you will build on these concepts and apply them to increasingly complex scenarios. You will learn how to structure deals that involve multiple entities, layered financing, and unique borrower situations. By mastering the architecture of advanced structuring, you position yourself to succeed at the highest levels of SBA commercial lending.

Real-Life Math Example: Structuring a Complex SBA Commercial Mortgage Deal

To fully understand advanced structuring, it is essential to see how these concepts apply in a real-world scenario. In this example, we will walk through a detailed SBA 7(a) loan structure for a borrower acquiring a business and the associated real estate. This example will demonstrate how financial adjustments, ownership structuring, and strategic planning can transform a deal into a strong, approvable transaction.

Consider a borrower named Michael who is purchasing a small manufacturing business along with the commercial property it operates in. The total purchase price is $2,000,000, with $1,400,000 allocated to real estate and $600,000 allocated to the business. Michael plans to use an SBA 7(a) loan to finance the transaction with a 10% down payment.

The total project cost is $2,000,000. Michael contributes $200,000 as a down payment, leaving a loan amount of $1,800,000. The interest rate is assumed to be 10% with a 25-year amortization for the real estate portion blended with a shorter term for the business portion, resulting in an estimated monthly payment of approximately $17,400.

Now we evaluate the business's financials. The business generates $500,000 in annual gross revenue. After expenses, the net income reported on tax returns is $120,000. However, upon closer analysis, several add-backs are identified. These include $40,000 in depreciation, $20,000 in owner discretionary expenses, and a one-time expense of $15,000. This results in an adjusted net income of:

$120,000 + $40,000 + $20,000 + $15,000 = $195,000

Next, we calculate the debt service coverage ratio (DSCR). The annual loan payment is:

$17,400 × 12 = $208,800

Now we divide the adjusted net income by the annual debt service:

$195,000 ÷ $208,800 ≈ 0.93

At this stage, the deal does not meet the typical SBA requirement of at least 1.25 DSCR. This is where advanced structuring comes into play.

To improve the DSCR, several strategies are considered. First, we explore increasing the down payment. If Michael increases his down payment to 15%, or $300,000, the loan amount decreases to $1,700,000. This reduces the monthly payment to approximately $16,400, resulting in an annual debt service of:

$16,400 × 12 = $196,800

Recalculating DSCR:

$195,000 ÷ $196,800 ≈ 0.99

Still not sufficient. Next, we consider restructuring the deal by introducing a seller note. The seller agrees to carry a $200,000 note on full standby for the first two years. This reduces the SBA loan amount to $1,600,000.

The new monthly payment is approximately $15,400, resulting in annual debt service of:

$15,400 × 12 = $184,800

Recalculating DSCR:

$195,000 ÷ $184,800 ≈ 1.06

We are getting closer, but still below the target.

Now, we further analyze the business and identify opportunities to increase revenue. The borrower provides a projection showing that minor operational improvements could increase annual revenue by $50,000 with minimal additional expenses. Assuming a conservative net increase of $30,000, the adjusted net income becomes:

$195,000 + $30,000 = $225,000

Now we recalculate DSCR:

$225,000 ÷ $184,800 ≈ 1.22

Finally, we introduce one more structuring element—additional collateral. Michael owns a residential property with significant equity, which he agrees to pledge as additional collateral. While this does not directly change

DSCR, it reduces lender risk and makes the deal more acceptable at a slightly lower DSCR.

Additionally, the lender agrees to stretch the amortization slightly within SBA guidelines, reducing the monthly payment to $14,900. The new annual debt service becomes:

$\$14,900 \times 12 = \$178,800$

Final DSCR:

$\$225,000 \div \$178,800 \approx 1.26$

Now the deal meets SBA requirements and is positioned for approval.

This example illustrates how advanced structuring transforms a deal. Initially, the transaction appeared unapprovable with a DSCR below 1.0. However, through strategic adjustments—including increasing the down payment, introducing a seller note, improving projected income, and adding collateral—the deal was successfully restructured into a strong, approvable transaction.

The key takeaway is that structuring is about flexibility and problem-solving. Each adjustment improved a specific aspect of the deal, and together they created a balanced and compelling loan package. This is the power of advanced SBA commercial mortgage loan structuring.

Chapter 2

Mastering Cash Flow Optimization and Debt Service Structuring in SBA Commercial Mortgage Loans

At the advanced level of SBA commercial mortgage lending, cash flow is not just a requirement—it is the centerpiece of the entire deal. Every decision made by an underwriter, credit committee, or lender ultimately ties back to one fundamental question: can this borrower comfortably repay the loan? While this may seem straightforward, the reality is that cash flow is rarely as simple as the numbers shown on a tax return. Advanced structuring requires a deep understanding of how to analyze, adjust, and present cash flow in a way that accurately reflects the true financial strength of a business while remaining compliant with SBA guidelines.

The first step in mastering cash flow optimization is understanding how lenders interpret financials. Most SBA lenders rely heavily on historical tax returns, typically reviewing the past two to three years of business performance. However, these tax returns often do not tell the full story. Business owners frequently minimize taxable income through deductions, depreciation, and discretionary expenses. While this may be beneficial for tax purposes, it can create challenges when applying for financing. Advanced structuring involves identifying legitimate adjustments, commonly known as add-backs, that can be used to present a more accurate picture of the business's true earnings.

Add-backs are one of the most powerful tools in cash flow structuring. These include non-cash expenses such as depreciation and amortization, one-time or extraordinary expenses, and discretionary costs that are not essential to the operation of the business. For example, expenses related to personal travel, excess owner compensation, or non-recurring repairs may be added back to net income. However, it is critical that all add-backs are well-documented and justifiable. Lenders will scrutinize these adjustments closely, and unsupported add-backs can weaken the credibility of the entire deal.

Another important aspect of cash flow optimization is normalization. This involves adjusting financials to reflect a stable and sustainable level of income. Businesses often experience fluctuations in revenue and expenses due to seasonal trends, market conditions, or one-time events. Advanced structuring requires analyzing these fluctuations and determining what represents the true ongoing performance of the business. This may involve averaging income over multiple years or excluding outlier periods that do not accurately represent normal operations.

Debt service coverage ratio (DSCR) remains the primary metric used to evaluate cash flow. At its core, DSCR measures the relationship between a business's available income and its debt obligations. While most lenders look for a minimum DSCR of 1.25, advanced structuring focuses on how to achieve and exceed this threshold through strategic adjustments. This includes not only increasing income but also reducing debt service through structuring techniques such as longer amortization periods, lower interest rates, or partial seller financing.

Debt structuring plays a crucial role in cash flow optimization. The terms of the loan—such as interest rate, amortization period, and repayment schedule—directly impact the monthly payment and, therefore, the DSCR. Advanced structuring involves negotiating and selecting loan terms that align with the borrower's cash flow while still meeting SBA and lender requirements. For example, extending the amortization period can significantly reduce monthly payments, improving DSCR and making the deal more attractive to lenders.

In addition to the primary loan, existing debt obligations must also be considered. Many borrowers have multiple loans, lines of credit, or other financial obligations that impact their overall cash flow. Advanced structuring involves analyzing these obligations and determining whether they can be refinanced, consolidated, or subordinated to improve the borrower's financial position. In some cases, restructuring existing debt can be the key to achieving an acceptable DSCR.

Revenue analysis is another critical component of cash flow optimization. Lenders want to see not only stable income but also the potential for growth. Advanced structuring involves identifying opportunities to increase revenue and presenting these opportunities in a credible and realistic manner. This may include expanding services, increasing pricing, or improving operational efficiency. While projections must be supported by data and reasonable assumptions, they can play an important role in strengthening a deal.

Expense management is equally important. Reducing unnecessary expenses can have a direct and immediate impact on cash flow. Advanced structuring involves reviewing all business expenses and identifying areas where costs can be reduced without negatively impacting operations. This may include renegotiating contracts, eliminating non-essential expenses, or improving operational efficiency. Even small reductions in expenses can significantly improve DSCR. Another advanced strategy is layering multiple sources of income. In some cases, borrowers may have additional income streams that can be included in the analysis. This could include rental income, secondary businesses, or other sources of revenue. Properly documenting and including these income streams can strengthen the overall cash flow profile and improve approval chances.

Working capital is often overlooked but plays a vital role in cash flow stability. Adequate working capital ensures that a business can handle short-term expenses and unexpected challenges. Advanced structuring involves ensuring that the borrower has sufficient working capital after closing, either through loan proceeds or existing reserves. This not only supports the business but also reassures lenders that the borrower is prepared for potential fluctuations in income.

Presentation is a key element of cash flow structuring. Even the strongest financials can be misunderstood if they are not presented clearly. Advanced structuring involves organizing financial information in a way that is easy for underwriters to understand. This includes providing detailed explanations for add-backs, clear summaries of financial performance, and supporting documentation for all adjustments. A well-presented file builds confidence and reduces the likelihood of delays or additional conditions. Risk mitigation remains a central theme throughout the structuring process.

Lenders are more likely to approve a deal when they perceive lower risk. By optimizing cash flow, reducing debt service, and presenting a clear and compelling financial narrative, advanced structuring minimizes perceived risk and increases approval likelihood. This proactive approach is what distinguishes top-performing loan professionals from the rest.

As you continue to develop your skills, you will begin to see cash flow not as a fixed number but as a dynamic component that can be shaped and optimized. This perspective allows you to approach each deal with creativity and confidence, knowing that there are multiple ways to achieve a strong and approvable structure. Mastering cash flow optimization is one of the most valuable skills in SBA commercial mortgage lending, and it will serve as the foundation for all advanced structuring strategies moving forward.

Real-Life Math Example: Cash Flow Optimization and DSCR Structuring

In this real-world scenario, we will walk through a detailed example of how cash flow optimization can transform a marginal SBA loan into a strong, approvable deal. This example will demonstrate how to analyze financials, apply add-backs, adjust loan terms, and strategically structure a transaction to meet SBA requirements. Consider a borrower named Sarah who owns a service-based business and is seeking an SBA 7(a) loan to purchase a commercial property for her operations. The total project cost is $1,500,000. Sarah plans to put down 10%, or $150,000, resulting in a loan amount of $1,350,000. The interest rate is 10%, and the loan is amortized over 25 years, resulting in a monthly payment of approximately $12,300.

The annual debt service is calculated as:

$12,300 × 12 = $147,600

Now we analyze the business's financials. Sarah's business generates $400,000 in annual revenue. After expenses, the net income reported on her tax returns is $100,000. At first glance, this appears insufficient to support the loan. However, a deeper analysis reveals several add-backs.

Depreciation: $25,000 Owner discretionary expenses: $15,000 One-time repair cost: $10,000

Adjusted net income:

$100,000 + $25,000 + $15,000 + $10,000 = $150,000

Now we calculate DSCR:

$150,000 ÷ $147,600 ≈ 1.02

This is below the typical requirement of 1.25, so the deal needs further structuring.

First, we explore reducing the loan amount by increasing the down payment. Sarah decides to increase her down payment to 15%, or $225,000. The new loan amount is $1,275,000. This reduces the monthly payment to approximately $11,600.

New annual debt service:

$11,600 × 12 = $139,200

Revised DSCR:

$150,000 ÷ $139,200 ≈ 1.08

Still not sufficient.

Next, we consider extending the amortization period within SBA guidelines, reducing the monthly payment to $11,000.

New annual debt service:

$11,000 × 12 = $132,000

Revised DSCR:

$150,000 ÷ $132,000 ≈ 1.14

We are getting closer, but still below target.

Now we analyze revenue growth opportunities. Sarah demonstrates that by adding a new service line, she can increase annual revenue by $60,000 with minimal additional expenses. Assuming a conservative net increase of $40,000, the adjusted net income becomes:

$150,000 + $40,000 = $190,000

Revised DSCR:

$190,000 ÷ $132,000 ≈ 1.44

At this point, the deal meets and exceeds SBA requirements.

To further strengthen the deal, Sarah agrees to maintain a working capital reserve of $50,000 after closing. This provides additional security for the lender and reduces perceived risk.

This example illustrates how multiple structuring strategies can be combined to optimize cash flow and achieve approval. By applying add-backs, increasing the down payment, adjusting loan terms, and incorporating realistic revenue growth, a marginal deal was transformed into a strong and approvable transaction.

The key takeaway is that cash flow is not static—it can be improved and optimized through strategic structuring. Understanding how to manipulate these variables within SBA guidelines is what allows you to consistently structure successful deals.

Chapter 3

Ownership Structures, Entity Design, and SBA Eligibility Optimization

At the advanced level of SBA commercial mortgage loan structuring, one of the most powerful—and often underutilized—tools is ownership and entity design. While many borrowers focus primarily on income, credit, and collateral, experienced professionals understand that how a deal is structured legally can significantly impact eligibility, approval likelihood, flexibility, and long-term wealth building. In many cases, deals are not declined because of weak financials, but because they are improperly structured from an ownership or entity standpoint. This chapter will guide you through how to strategically design ownership structures and entities to align with SBA requirements while maximizing deal strength and scalability.

The foundation of SBA ownership structuring begins with understanding eligibility. The SBA requires that borrowers meet specific criteria, including being for-profit entities, operating within the United States, and falling within size standards. However, beyond these basic requirements, ownership becomes critical. Generally, any individual who owns 20% or more of the borrowing entity must provide a full personal guarantee. This rule alone has major implications when structuring partnerships, bringing in investors, or allocating ownership across multiple parties.

Advanced structuring begins by recognizing that ownership percentages are not just arbitrary—they can be strategically designed. For example, if a borrower wants to include a partner who does not have strong credit or financials, structuring that partner below the 20% threshold may eliminate the need for their guarantee. Conversely, including a strong financial partner above 20% can enhance the strength of the deal. This level of intentional ownership design allows you to shape the borrower profile presented to the lender.

Entity structuring is equally important. In many SBA commercial real estate transactions, two primary entities are used: an operating company (OpCo) and a real estate holding company (PropCo). The operating company runs the business and generates revenue, while the real estate entity owns the property and leases it to the operating company. This structure provides several advantages, including liability protection, tax planning flexibility, and compliance with SBA requirements when properly executed.

The lease between the operating company and the real estate entity must meet SBA standards, particularly in owner-occupied transactions where at least 51% of the property is used by the business. Advanced structuring ensures that this lease is properly documented, reflects market terms, and aligns with lender expectations. Improper lease structuring can lead to delays or even denial, making this a critical component of the overall deal.

Affiliation rules are another key consideration in ownership structuring. The SBA evaluates not only the borrowing entity but also affiliated businesses when determining eligibility. Affiliation can be created through ownership, management control, or even contractual relationships. Advanced structuring involves identifying potential affiliations early and structuring ownership in a way that minimizes negative impacts. This may include separating entities, adjusting ownership percentages, or restructuring management roles.

Another powerful strategy involves layering ownership across multiple entities. For example, a borrower may own multiple businesses or properties through separate entities that are all connected through a holding company. This allows for centralized control while maintaining separation for liability and operational purposes. When structured correctly, this approach can support scalability and make it easier to acquire additional properties or businesses using SBA financing. Personal guarantees are a central component of SBA loans, and structuring them strategically is essential. While all owners above 20% are typically required to guarantee the loan, advanced structuring may involve including additional guarantors who strengthen the deal. This could include spouses, partners, or even key stakeholders who bring financial strength to the transaction. The goal is to present a strong guarantor profile that reassures the lender.

Another advanced concept is succession and transition structuring. Many SBA loans involve business acquisitions or ownership transitions. Structuring these deals correctly ensures continuity and stability. This may involve gradual ownership transfers, seller participation, or structured buyouts. These strategies not only improve approval chances but also create smoother transitions for the business.

Tax considerations also play a role in entity structuring. Different entity types—such as LLCs, S corporations, and partnerships—have different tax implications. Advanced structuring involves selecting the appropriate entity type based on the borrower's goals, financial situation, and long-term plans. While tax advice should be coordinated with a CPA, understanding these implications allows you to structure deals more effectively. Control and decision-making authority are additional factors to consider. Lenders want to see that the individuals responsible for the business have the authority to make decisions and manage operations effectively. Structuring ownership in a way that clearly defines control can strengthen the deal. This includes outlining roles, responsibilities, and decision-making processes within the entity.

Another important aspect is scalability. Advanced structuring is not just about the current deal—it is about positioning the borrower for future growth. This means creating an entity structure that can support additional acquisitions, expansions, and financing opportunities. By thinking ahead, you can avoid the need to restructure entities later, saving time and reducing complexity.

Documentation is critical in ownership and entity structuring. Lenders require clear and accurate documentation of ownership percentages, entity relationships, and operating agreements. Advanced structuring involves preparing these documents in a way that is both compliant and easy to understand. Clear documentation reduces confusion and builds confidence with underwriters.

As you develop your structuring skills, you will begin to see ownership and entity design as powerful tools rather than administrative requirements. These elements allow you to shape the deal, control risk, and create opportunities that would not otherwise exist. Mastering this aspect of structuring is essential for handling complex SBA transactions and building a scalable real estate and business portfolio.

Ultimately, ownership and entity structuring is about alignment. It is about aligning the borrower's goals with SBA guidelines, lender expectations, and long-term strategy. When done correctly, it creates a strong foundation for the entire deal and significantly increases the likelihood of approval.

Real-Life Math Example: Ownership Structuring and Its Impact on SBA Loan Approval

To understand how ownership structuring affects SBA loan approval, let's walk through a detailed real-world scenario involving multiple partners, entity structuring, and financial impact.

Consider a deal where three partners—John, Lisa, and Mark—are purchasing a commercial property and operating business for $1,800,000. The structure initially is:

John: 50% ownership Lisa: 30% ownership Mark: 20% ownership

The loan amount is $1,620,000 with a 10% down payment of $180,000. The estimated monthly payment is $14,800, resulting in annual debt service of:

$14,800 × 12 = $177,600

The business generates adjusted net income of $210,000. The DSCR is:

$210,000 ÷ $177,600 ≈ 1.18

This is slightly below the preferred 1.25 threshold.

Now we evaluate the partners individually. John and Lisa have strong credit and financial profiles, but Mark has weak credit and limited financial strength. Because Mark owns 20%, he is required to provide a personal guarantee, which weakens the overall borrower profile.

To improve the deal, we restructure ownership:

John: 55% Lisa: 35% Mark: 10%

By reducing Mark's ownership below 20%, he is no longer required to guarantee the loan. This strengthens the guarantor profile significantly.

Next, we introduce an additional strategy. Lisa agrees to inject an additional $50,000 into the deal, increasing the total down payment to $230,000. This reduces the loan amount to $1,570,000.

The new monthly payment is approximately $14,200, resulting

in annual debt service of:

$14,200 × 12 = $170,400

Revised DSCR:

$210,000 ÷ $170,400 ≈ 1.23

Still slightly below target.

Now we incorporate a seller note of $100,000 on standby, reducing the SBA loan amount to $1,470,000.

The new monthly payment is approximately $13,300, resulting in annual debt service of:

$13,300 × 12 = $159,600

Revised DSCR:

$210,000 ÷ $159,600 ≈ 1.32

Now the deal exceeds SBA requirements.

Additionally, by structuring the entities properly, the partners create two entities:

Operating Company (OpCo): owned by John (55%), Lisa (35%), Mark (10%) Real Estate Holding Company (PropCo): owned by John (60%), Lisa (40%)

Mark is excluded from the real estate entity, simplifying the structure and reducing risk.

The lease between OpCo and PropCo is structured at market rates, ensuring compliance with SBA guidelines and supporting cash flow analysis.

This example demonstrates how ownership structuring directly impacts loan approval. By adjusting ownership percentages, removing a weak guarantor, increasing equity injection, and introducing a seller note, the deal was transformed from marginal to strong.

The key takeaway is that ownership is not just about who owns what—it is a strategic tool that can be used to strengthen a deal, reduce risk, and improve approval chances. Mastering this concept allows you to structure more complex and successful SBA transactions.

Chapter 4

Advanced Risk Mitigation and Lender Psychology in SBA Commercial Mortgage Structuring

At the highest level of SBA commercial mortgage lending, structuring is no longer just about numbers—it is about perception. Every deal is evaluated not only on its financial strength but on how risky it appears to the lender. Understanding and controlling this perception is what separates average loan submissions from consistently approved, high-level transactions. This chapter focuses on advanced risk mitigation and the psychology behind lender decision-making, giving you the tools to structure deals that not only meet guidelines but feel safe and compelling to approve.

Lenders are not simply analyzing data; they are making judgment calls based on patterns, experience, and internal risk tolerance. Even when two deals have identical numbers, one may be approved while the other is declined based on how the story is presented. This is where advanced structuring becomes critical. Your job is to identify every potential weakness in a deal and proactively address it before it becomes an objection. This requires thinking like an underwriter and anticipating the questions they will ask.

The first step in risk mitigation is identifying the core risk categories within a deal. These typically include borrower risk, business risk, property risk, and market risk. Borrower risk relates to credit history, experience, and financial strength. Business risk involves the stability and profitability of the business. Property risk considers the value, condition, and marketability of the real estate. Market risk evaluates broader economic and local market conditions. Advanced structuring involves analyzing each of these categories and ensuring that strengths in one area compensate for weaknesses in another.

Borrower strength is one of the most influential factors in lender psychology. A borrower with strong credit, liquidity, and experience immediately reduces perceived risk. However, not every borrower fits this ideal profile. Advanced structuring involves enhancing borrower strength through strategic positioning. This may include adding a co-borrower, strengthening liquidity through reserves, or highlighting relevant experience that supports the business's success. Even small improvements in borrower profile can have a significant impact on approval likelihood.

Liquidity is a key component of borrower strength and risk mitigation. Lenders want to see that borrowers have sufficient reserves to handle unexpected challenges. Advanced structuring involves ensuring that borrowers maintain adequate liquidity after closing. This may include structuring the deal to leave cash in the business, setting aside working capital, or documenting additional sources of funds. Strong liquidity not only improves approval chances but also provides a safety net for the borrower.

Experience is another critical factor in lender decision-making. Lenders prefer borrowers who have experience in the industry they are entering. If a borrower lacks direct experience, advanced structuring involves bridging this gap. This could include bringing in a partner with relevant experience, highlighting transferable skills, or providing a detailed business plan that demonstrates competence and preparation. The goal is to reduce uncertainty and build confidence in the borrower's ability to succeed.

Business stability is closely tied to risk perception. Lenders favor businesses with consistent revenue, strong customer bases, and predictable cash flow. Advanced structuring involves presenting the business in a way that emphasizes these strengths. This includes providing detailed financial analysis, demonstrating revenue trends, and explaining any fluctuations. Stability reduces perceived risk and makes the deal more attractive to lenders. Property risk is another important consideration. The type, condition, and location of the property all influence lender decisions. Advanced structuring involves selecting properties that align with lender preferences and presenting them effectively. This may include obtaining high-quality appraisals, providing market data, and highlighting features that enhance value and marketability. A strong property reduces risk and supports the overall structure of the deal.

Market conditions also play a role in lender psychology. Economic trends, local market dynamics, and industry conditions can all impact how a deal is perceived. Advanced structuring involves understanding these factors and positioning the deal accordingly. For example, demonstrating strong demand in the local market or highlighting industry growth trends can help offset other risks.

Another powerful risk mitigation strategy is the use of compensating factors. These are strengths that offset weaknesses in a deal. For example, a slightly lower DSCR may be acceptable if the borrower has strong liquidity, excellent credit, or significant industry experience. Advanced structuring involves identifying and emphasizing these compensating factors to create a balanced and compelling deal. Collateral is often used as a secondary risk mitigation tool. While SBA loans are primarily cash flow-driven, additional collateral can provide lenders with added security. Advanced structuring involves using collateral strategically, ensuring that it supports the deal without overcomplicating the structure. Properly used, collateral can make the difference in borderline cases.

Another critical aspect of lender psychology is clarity. Underwriters are more likely to approve deals that are easy to understand. Confusion creates risk. Advanced structuring involves presenting the deal in a clear, organized, and logical manner. This includes summarizing key points, providing detailed explanations, and ensuring that all documentation is complete and consistent. A clear presentation builds confidence and reduces the likelihood of additional conditions.

Narrative plays a significant role in how a deal is perceived. Every transaction tells a story, and advanced structuring involves crafting that story in a way that resonates with lenders. This includes explaining the borrower's background, the business's performance, and the purpose of the loan. A strong narrative ties all elements of the deal together and makes it easier for lenders to justify approval.

Proactive problem-solving is another hallmark of advanced

structuring. Instead of waiting for lenders to identify issues, you address them upfront. This may involve providing explanations for credit issues, documenting unusual financials, or outlining plans to mitigate risks. By addressing concerns early, you reduce uncertainty and build trust with the lender.

Consistency across all aspects of the deal is essential. Inconsistencies create red flags and increase perceived risk. Advanced structuring involves ensuring that all information—financials, applications, narratives, and documentation—aligns perfectly. This attention to detail demonstrates professionalism and reliability.

As you master these concepts, you will begin to see deals through the lens of risk and perception. You will understand not only what lenders are looking for but why they are looking for it. This insight allows you to structure deals that align with lender psychology, increasing approval rates and creating smoother transactions.

Ultimately, advanced risk mitigation is about control. It is about controlling how a deal is perceived and ensuring that every element works together to create confidence. By mastering this skill, you position yourself to handle even the most complex SBA commercial mortgage transactions with clarity and precision.

Real-Life Math Example: Risk Mitigation and Structuring for Approval

In this example, we will demonstrate how advanced risk mitigation strategies can transform a borderline SBA loan into a strong, approvable deal by addressing lender concerns and improving overall perception.

Consider a borrower named David who is purchasing a commercial property and business for $2,200,000. He plans to use an SBA loan with a 10% down payment of $220,000, resulting in a loan amount of $1,980,000. The interest rate is 10%, and the monthly payment is approximately $18,000.

Annual debt service:

$\$18{,}000 \times 12 = \$216{,}000$

The business generates adjusted net income of $250,000. Initial DSCR:

$\$250{,}000 \div \$216{,}000 \approx 1.16$

This is below the preferred 1.25 threshold, making the deal borderline.

First, we identify key risks:

- DSCR below target
- Limited liquidity after closing
- Moderate credit score (680)
- Limited industry experience

Now we begin structuring solutions.

Step 1: Increase Down Payment David increases his down payment by $80,000, bringing total equity to $300,000. The loan amount decreases to $1,900,000.

New monthly payment: $17,200 Annual debt service:

$17,200 × 12 = $206,400

New DSCR:

$250,000 ÷ $206,400 ≈ 1.21

Step 2: Seller Note on Standby The seller agrees to carry a $150,000 note on standby, reducing the SBA loan to $1,750,000.

New monthly payment: $15,800 Annual debt service:

$15,800 × 12 = $189,600

New DSCR:

$250,000 ÷ $189,600 ≈ 1.32

Step 3: Liquidity Improvement David maintains $100,000 in reserves after closing. While this does not change DSCR, it significantly reduces lender risk.

Step 4: Add Experienced Partner David brings in a partner with 25% ownership who has 10 years of experience in the industry. This strengthens the borrower profile and offsets David's lack of experience.

Step 5: Additional Collateral David pledges a rental property with $200,000 in equity, further reducing lender risk.

Step 6: Revenue Stabilization Financial analysis shows consistent revenue over the past three years, reinforcing business stability.

Final Outcome:

Adjusted loan amount: $1,750,000 Annual debt service: $189,600 Adjusted net income: $250,000 Final DSCR:

$250,000 ÷ $189,600 ≈ 1.32

Through strategic risk mitigation—improving DSCR, increasing liquidity, adding experience, and strengthening collateral—the deal is transformed from borderline to strong.

This example highlights a key principle: lenders do not expect perfect deals, but they do expect well-structured ones. By addressing risks proactively and presenting a balanced, compelling transaction, you significantly increase the likelihood of approval.

Chapter 5

Advanced Use of Proceeds Structuring and Multi-Purpose SBA Loan Design

At the advanced level of SBA commercial mortgage loan structuring, one of the most powerful and often overlooked strategies is how the use of proceeds is designed within a transaction. While many borrowers and even loan professionals think of SBA loans in simple terms—buying a property or acquiring a business—the reality is that SBA financing allows for highly flexible, multi-purpose structures that can dramatically increase the value of a deal. The way funds are allocated can directly impact approval, cash flow, scalability, and long-term profitability. This chapter focuses on mastering the art of structuring use of proceeds to maximize both approval chances and financial outcomes.

The foundation of advanced use of proceeds structuring begins with understanding what the SBA allows. SBA loans can be used for a wide range of purposes, including real estate acquisition, business acquisition, partner buyouts, refinancing existing debt, equipment purchases, construction, renovations, and working capital. However, simply knowing these categories is not enough. Advanced structuring involves combining multiple uses into a single, cohesive transaction that aligns with both SBA guidelines and lender preferences.

One of the key advantages of SBA loans is the ability to consolidate multiple financial needs into one loan. Instead of obtaining separate financing for real estate, equipment, and working capital, borrowers can structure a single SBA loan that covers all these components. This not only simplifies the financing process but also improves cash flow by creating a single, manageable monthly payment. Advanced structuring involves determining the optimal allocation of funds across these categories to achieve the best overall outcome.

Working capital is one of the most critical components of use of proceeds structuring. While it may not generate immediate returns like real estate or equipment, it plays a vital role in ensuring business stability and growth. Advanced structuring involves including sufficient working capital in the loan to support operations, cover initial expenses, and provide a buffer for unexpected challenges. Lenders view adequate working capital as a positive factor because it reduces the risk of cash flow disruptions.

Another important aspect is the strategic allocation between hard assets and operational funding. Real estate and equipment are tangible assets that provide collateral and long-term value, while working capital and business acquisition costs support operations and growth. Advanced structuring involves balancing these components to create a deal that is both secure and profitable. Too much emphasis on one category can create weaknesses, while a well-balanced structure enhances overall strength.

Refinancing existing debt is another powerful use of proceeds strategy. Many borrowers enter SBA transactions with existing loans that carry high interest rates or unfavorable terms. By incorporating debt refinancing into the SBA loan, borrowers can reduce their overall debt burden, lower monthly payments, and improve cash flow. Advanced structuring involves identifying which debts can be refinanced under SBA guidelines and integrating them into the new loan in a way that strengthens the overall deal.

Partner buyouts and ownership transitions also play a significant role in advanced structuring. SBA loans can be used to buy out existing partners or restructure ownership within a business. This creates opportunities for borrowers to gain full control of their business or bring in new partners strategically. Structuring these transactions correctly ensures compliance with SBA rules while supporting long-term business goals.

Construction and renovation components add another layer of complexity to use of proceeds structuring. When a deal involves building or improving a property, funds must be allocated carefully to cover all aspects of the project, including materials, labor, permits, and contingencies. Advanced structuring involves planning these costs in detail and ensuring that sufficient funds are available to complete the project without delays or cost overruns.

Timing and sequencing of fund disbursement are also critical. Not all funds in an SBA loan are disbursed at closing. Some, such as construction or working capital, may be released in stages. Advanced structuring involves planning how and when funds will be used to support the borrower's operations and project timelines. Proper sequencing ensures that the business has the resources it needs at each stage of the transaction.

Another advanced concept is leveraging use of proceeds to improve DSCR and overall deal strength. For example, using a portion of the loan to refinance high-interest debt can reduce monthly obligations, thereby improving cash flow and DSCR. Similarly, allocating funds toward revenue-generating improvements can increase income and strengthen the deal. These strategies demonstrate how use of proceeds is not just about spending money—it is about strategically deploying capital to enhance the financial profile of the transaction. Lender preferences also play a role in how use of proceeds is structured. Some lenders may favor certain types of transactions, such as owner-occupied real estate or stable business acquisitions. Advanced structuring involves aligning the use of proceeds with lender preferences to increase approval likelihood. This requires understanding the lending landscape and tailoring the deal accordingly.

Documentation and clarity are essential in use of proceeds structuring. Lenders require detailed breakdowns of how funds will be used, and any ambiguity can create delays or concerns. Advanced structuring involves preparing clear and comprehensive documentation that outlines each component of the loan and its purpose. This level of detail builds confidence and facilitates smoother underwriting.

Another important consideration is long-term strategy. The way funds are used in the initial transaction can impact future opportunities. Advanced structuring involves thinking beyond the immediate deal and considering how the use of proceeds will position the borrower for growth. This may include preserving capital for future investments, improving operational efficiency, or creating opportunities for expansion.

As you develop your expertise, you will begin to see use of proceeds as a strategic tool rather than a simple requirement. It becomes a way to shape the deal, optimize financial performance, and create opportunities that extend far beyond the initial transaction. Mastering this aspect of structuring allows you to design deals that are not only approvable but also highly effective in achieving the borrower's goals.

Ultimately, advanced use of proceeds structuring is about maximizing the impact of every dollar. It is about ensuring that funds are allocated in a way that strengthens the deal, supports the business, and creates long-term value. By mastering this skill, you position yourself to structure more complex, flexible, and profitable SBA commercial mortgage transactions.

Real-Life Math Example: Multi-Purpose SBA Loan Structuring and Use of Proceeds Optimization

In this example, we will walk through a detailed SBA loan structure that combines multiple uses of proceeds, demonstrating how strategic allocation can improve cash flow, DSCR, and overall deal strength.

Consider a borrower named Alex who is acquiring a business and commercial property for a total project cost of $2,500,000. The breakdown is as follows:

Real estate purchase: $1,600,000 Business acquisition: $600,000 Equipment upgrades: $100,000 Working capital: $200,000

Total project cost: $2,500,000

Alex contributes a 10% down payment of $250,000, resulting in a loan amount of $2,250,000. The interest rate is 10%, and the monthly payment is approximately $20,500.

Annual debt service:

$20,500 × 12 = $246,000

The business generates adjusted net income of $280,000. Initial DSCR:

$280,000 ÷ $246,000 ≈ 1.14

This is below the preferred 1.25 threshold.

Now we begin optimizing the structure.

Step 1: Refinance Existing Debt The business currently has an existing loan with a monthly payment of $3,000 ($36,000 annually). By refinancing this debt into the SBA loan, we eliminate this obligation.

Adjusted available cash flow:

$280,000 + $36,000 = $316,000

New DSCR:

$316,000 ÷ $246,000 ≈ 1.28

Now the deal meets SBA requirements.

Step 2: Adjust Working Capital Allocation Instead of allocating $200,000 to working capital, we reduce it to $150,000 and increase the down payment by $50,000.

New loan amount:

$2,200,000

New monthly payment: $20,000 Annual debt service:

$20,000 × 12 = $240,000

Revised DSCR:

$316,000 ÷ $240,000 ≈ 1.32

Step 3: Equipment Investment Impact The $100,000 equipment upgrade is expected to increase annual revenue by $80,000 with minimal additional expenses. Assuming a net increase of $50,000:

New adjusted income:

$316,000 + $50,000 = $366,000

Revised DSCR:

$366,000 ÷ $240,000 ≈ 1.53

Step 4: Seller Note Introduction The seller agrees to carry a $200,000 note on standby, reducing the SBA loan amount to $2,000,000.

New monthly payment: $18,200 Annual debt service:

$18,200 × 12 = $218,400

Final DSCR:

$366,000 ÷ $218,400 ≈ 1.68

Final Structure Summary:

Loan amount: $2,000,000 Down payment: $300,000 Seller note: $200,000 (standby) Annual income: $366,000 Annual debt service: $218,400 Final DSCR: 1.68

This example demonstrates how advanced use of proceeds structuring can dramatically improve a deal. By refinancing existing debt, adjusting working capital, investing in revenue-generating equipment, and introducing a seller note, the deal was transformed from borderline to exceptionally strong.

The key takeaway is that how funds are used is just as important as how much is borrowed. Strategic allocation of proceeds can improve cash flow, reduce risk, and create a more compelling loan structure that is highly likely to be approved.

Chapter 6

Structuring SBA Commercial Mortgage Loans with Seller Financing, Equity Injection, and Layered Capital

As SBA commercial mortgage transactions become more advanced, one of the most valuable skills a borrower, broker, lender, or investor can develop is the ability to structure layered capital. In simple deals, the financing stack may involve only two parts: the borrower's down payment and the SBA loan. But in more sophisticated transactions, the strongest deals are often built with multiple capital layers working together in a strategic way. These layers may include borrower equity, seller financing, standby notes, gift funds where permitted, investor contributions, and retained business liquidity. Understanding how to combine these elements properly can improve cash flow, increase approval odds, reduce lender risk, preserve borrower liquidity, and help close deals that would otherwise fall apart. This chapter explores how to structure SBA commercial mortgage loans using seller financing, equity injection, and layered capital in a way that is both compliant and highly effective. The first principle to understand is that capital stack design directly affects risk. Lenders are always trying to answer the same core question: how much real commitment does the borrower have in the deal, and how much protection exists if the deal underperforms? A borrower who contributes meaningful equity demonstrates commitment and reduces the lender's exposure. A seller who carries financing demonstrates confidence in the business or property being sold. Additional reserves left in the business after closing improve stability. When these elements are structured correctly, the transaction becomes stronger from every angle. Advanced structuring is not simply about coming up with enough money to close. It is about designing the capital stack to tell a story of strength, alignment, and reduced risk.

Equity injection is one of the most scrutinized parts of any SBA transaction. At a basic level, borrowers know they usually need to bring a percentage of the total project cost into the deal. But advanced structuring goes much deeper. It involves deciding where that equity comes from, when it is contributed, how it is documented, and how it interacts with the rest of the capital stack. Some borrowers make the mistake of putting all available cash into the down payment, leaving themselves with little working capital after closing. Others try to minimize their injection too aggressively, which weakens the file and creates underwriting concerns. The best structures achieve balance. They satisfy lender requirements while preserving enough liquidity to support the business after the loan funds. One of the strongest tools in advanced SBA structuring is seller financing. In many business acquisition or mixed business and real estate transactions, the seller is willing to carry a note for part of the purchase price. This can be extraordinarily valuable when structured correctly. Seller financing can reduce the amount of SBA debt needed, lower monthly debt service, improve debt service coverage ratios, and reduce the borrower's required cash contribution in some cases depending on how the note is documented and whether it is placed on full standby. It can also signal to the lender that the seller believes in the continuing viability of the business. However, not all seller notes are created equal. Some count against cash flow immediately, while others do not. Some strengthen the deal, while others complicate it. The details matter.

Full standby is one of the most important concepts when using seller financing. A seller note placed on full standby means no principal or interest payments are due for a certain period, often at least two years depending on lender and SBA structure. When a seller note is on full standby and properly documented, it may help satisfy part of the equity injection requirement and may not need to be counted in immediate debt service calculations. This can transform a marginal deal into an approvable one. In advanced structuring, a standby seller note is not just a financing convenience. It is a strategic instrument that enhances cash flow and lowers perceived risk. Another layer of sophistication comes from understanding the psychology of each capital source. Borrower cash shows commitment. Seller financing shows confidence. Investor capital shows support. Retained liquidity shows prudence. Together, these create a stronger narrative than any one source alone. Lenders want to see that the borrower is not overextended, that the seller still has some belief in the transaction, and that the business will not be left financially drained after closing. A well-layered capital stack creates exactly that impression. It demonstrates that the deal has been thoughtfully designed, that everyone involved has something at stake, and that the business has room to operate safely after funding.

There is also an important difference between simply filling a financing gap and strategically structuring layered capital. A weakly structured deal may use multiple capital sources in a desperate attempt to make the numbers work. A strong deal uses those same tools intentionally to create stability and strength. For example, instead of using every available dollar to increase the down payment, an advanced structure may combine a moderate borrower injection, a full standby seller note, and retained cash reserves. This may yield a better outcome than a larger borrower injection alone because the borrower remains more liquid and the business remains more resilient. In many cases, over-injecting cash can actually weaken the deal by leaving the borrower with too little flexibility after closing.

The structure of the purchase itself also matters greatly. In a business acquisition with commercial real estate, the total project cost may include the purchase price, closing costs, renovations, equipment, and working capital. Advanced capital stacking requires understanding which sources can be used for which components. Borrower cash may go toward required equity injection and closing costs. Seller financing may help bridge valuation gaps or reduce SBA exposure. The SBA loan may fund the bulk of the acquisition and eligible associated costs. When these layers are aligned correctly, the deal becomes smoother and more efficient. When they are mismatched, the file can become confusing and difficult to underwrite.

Seller notes are especially powerful in transactions where a business has strong potential but slightly weak historical cash flow. If a borrower is acquiring a company with a decent but not perfect DSCR, reducing the SBA loan amount through seller carry can significantly lower annual debt service. This may be enough to move the file above minimum coverage thresholds. At the same time, the seller note can help reassure the lender that the seller is not simply walking away, but remains financially tied to the business's continued success. That alignment of incentives is often highly persuasive in underwriting. Advanced structuring also requires careful attention to how equity is seasoned and documented. Lenders want to know where the borrower's funds came from, whether they are borrowed, and whether they are truly available. Large recent deposits may need to be explained. Transfers between accounts may need to be traced. If family support or partner contributions are involved, those must be documented clearly and properly. Even a strong deal can be delayed or weakened if the equity story is messy. One hallmark of advanced loan structuring is that the capital sources are not only strong, but also clean and easy to verify.

Layered capital becomes even more important when the borrower wants to preserve flexibility for growth. A business owner who uses every available dollar to close one transaction may not have the resources to handle repairs, marketing, payroll growth, or future opportunities. An advanced structure recognizes that approval is only the beginning. The borrower must be positioned to succeed after closing. This is why retained liquidity is such a powerful hidden factor in strong SBA deals. Lenders may not always state it directly, but they are far more comfortable approving a transaction when the borrower will still have meaningful reserves. Preserved liquidity helps the borrower survive normal business volatility and signals mature financial management. Another advanced strategy is using seller financing not just to reduce the loan amount, but to solve specific approval obstacles. For example, if appraisal support is slightly weak, a seller note may help bridge a valuation challenge without forcing the lender to overfinance. If a borrower is short on cash injection, a properly structured standby seller note may satisfy part of the equity requirement. If the business has strong upside but current historical earnings are slightly thin, reducing first-position SBA debt may make coverage work. In each of these cases, seller carry is not generic. It is targeted. It is used to solve a particular underwriting issue.

The interaction between equity injection and debt service is one of the most important math relationships in the capital stack. Every dollar that reduces the senior SBA loan can reduce monthly payments. Lower payments improve DSCR. Stronger DSCR improves approval likelihood. At the same time, every dollar of borrower cash used for injection is a dollar no longer available as reserve capital. Advanced structuring is about finding the point where the debt payment is low enough and post-close liquidity is still strong enough. This balance is rarely accidental. It is designed.

Some advanced deals also involve minority investors or partners contributing capital. In these situations, ownership structure, guarantor requirements, and affiliated interests must all be evaluated carefully. Investor capital can strengthen a deal significantly, but only when the ownership and documentation are structured properly. The presence of outside capital should make the deal simpler and stronger, not more confusing. A clean ownership table, clear operating agreement, and obvious explanation of who is contributing what and why are all essential.

In more complex transactions, capital layering can also be used to sequence risk. The borrower may bring in enough cash to show commitment, the seller may subordinate and stand by a note to support the transition, and the lender may fund the senior debt based on stabilized projected performance. Each layer absorbs risk differently. The borrower absorbs first-loss risk through cash injection. The seller absorbs some transition risk by waiting to be paid. The lender funds the core transaction with the protection of collateral, cash flow, and layered support beneath and around it. This is the kind of structure that sophisticated underwriters appreciate because it shows that risk has been distributed thoughtfully.

Documentation remains one of the most overlooked parts of layered-capital structuring. A great structure can be undermined by weak paperwork. Seller notes must be drafted clearly. Standby terms must be explicit. Source of funds documentation must be complete. Equity transfers must be traceable. Ownership contributions must match the legal agreements. The file narrative must explain the structure in plain language. When this is done well, the underwriter does not have to guess what is happening. They can immediately see how the transaction works and why it is strong. That clarity alone often improves the path to approval.

Ultimately, mastering seller financing, equity injection, and layered capital is about becoming a financial designer rather than a passive participant. Instead of accepting a transaction's raw numbers at face value, you learn how to reshape the deal so that each piece supports the others. You create a structure where borrower commitment, seller confidence, cash flow performance, and lender protection all align. This does not just increase the chance of approval. It increases the chance of long-term success. A well-capitalized, well-structured SBA transaction gives the borrower room to operate, room to grow, and room to recover from normal business challenges. That is the true goal of advanced SBA commercial mortgage structuring.

When you master this skill, you stop seeing down payments and seller notes as isolated items. You begin seeing the whole capital stack as a living system. Each piece affects leverage, cash flow, risk, approval, and post-closing strength. The strongest deals are rarely the simplest. They are the ones where each layer of capital has been placed with intention. In advanced SBA lending, that level of intentionality is what separates a file that merely gets submitted from a file that gets approved and performs well long after closing.

Real-Life Math Example: Using Seller Financing, Equity Injection, and Layered Capital to Rescue a Complex SBA Deal

To understand how layered capital works in a real-world SBA commercial mortgage transaction, let us walk through a detailed example involving a borrower purchasing a business and the real estate it occupies. This example will show how the transaction evolves from a weak, barely workable file into a strong, lender-friendly structure through strategic use of borrower cash, seller carry, and preserved reserves.

Imagine a borrower named Daniel who wants to acquire a specialty automotive service business and the commercial building where it operates. The total transaction includes several components. The real estate is priced at $1,450,000. The business is priced at $650,000. Closing costs and fees are estimated at $50,000. Initial equipment improvements needed in the first three months are projected at $75,000. Daniel also wants $75,000 of working capital available after closing to ensure smooth operations during the transition. The total project cost is therefore calculated as follows:

Real estate purchase: $1,450,000 Business purchase: $650,000 Closing costs: $50,000 Equipment improvements: $75,000 Working capital: $75,000

Total project cost = $2,300,000

Daniel initially believes he can solve the deal with a standard 10% injection and one SBA loan. Ten percent of $2,300,000 is $230,000. He has $260,000 in liquid funds, so on paper, he appears ready. That would leave a gross loan amount of $2,070,000 before any other adjustments. Assume the lender is offering a blended effective rate that produces an estimated monthly payment of $18,900 on the senior debt. The annual debt service would then be:

$18,900 x 12 = $226,800 annual debt service

Now we review the business cash flow. The business's most recent tax-return-adjusted cash flow is $255,000. After reviewing the financials, the lender allows legitimate add-backs totaling $20,000, bringing adjusted business cash flow to:

$255,000 + $20,000 = $275,000 adjusted cash flow

The initial debt service coverage ratio is:

$275,000 / $226,800 = 1.21 DSCR

At first glance, 1.21 may not look terrible, but many lenders on a deal of this size will want to see 1.25 or better, especially in a transition scenario where a new owner is taking over operations. There is another problem as well. If Daniel contributes $230,000 and also needs closing liquidity, equipment money, and working capital, his remaining personal reserves will be nearly exhausted. That weakens the file. The lender now sees two issues at once: the DSCR is slightly thin, and post-close liquidity is too tight.

This is where advanced structuring begins. Instead of trying to force the deal through with only borrower cash and senior debt, the capital stack is redesigned. First, the seller is asked to carry a note for $200,000. The seller agrees, but only if the note bears interest and is repaid later. To help the SBA structure, the note is placed on full standby for the first 24 months. That means Daniel does not have to make principal or interest payments on that seller note during the critical early transition period. Because of the standby treatment, the seller note does not hit immediate debt service the same way a fully amortizing note would.

Now the capital stack is revised. Instead of the SBA lender financing $2,070,000, the senior loan is reduced by the seller carry amount:

Original needed senior debt: $2,070,000 Less seller standby note: $200,000 New senior SBA loan: $1,870,000

Assume this reduced senior loan now carries an estimated monthly payment of $17,100. Annual debt service becomes:

$17,100 x 12 = $205,200 annual debt service

Now let us recalculate DSCR using the same adjusted business cash flow of $275,000:

$275,000 / $205,200 = 1.34 DSCR

That one change alone takes the file from 1.21 to 1.34, which is a major improvement. But the benefits do not stop there. Because the seller note is on full standby, the lender sees additional support in the transaction. The seller remains financially tied to the business and is not demanding immediate payment. This lowers perceived risk during transition.

Next, we revisit Daniel's equity injection. He still has $260,000 in liquid funds, but now the structure has more flexibility. Rather than forcing him to contribute every dollar needed up front in the most aggressive way possible, the new plan is designed to preserve cash. Daniel contributes $230,000 toward the project costs, satisfying the core injection requirement. That leaves him with:

\$260,000 - \$230,000 = \$30,000 remaining personal liquidity

That is still a bit light. So the lender and borrower explore an additional adjustment. Instead of financing the full \$75,000 of planned working capital inside the project, they reduce immediate working capital in the loan budget to \$50,000 and Daniel agrees to retain \$25,000 from his own post-close funds inside the business account. This means the business still starts with the same total practical liquidity, but the structure is cleaner and Daniel's remaining cash position is easier to explain.

Let us update the project cost slightly:

Original working capital budget: \$75,000 Revised loan-funded working capital: \$50,000 Reduction in project cost: \$25,000

Revised total project cost = \$2,300,000 - \$25,000 = \$2,275,000

Now if Daniel still contributes \$230,000 and the seller carries \$200,000, the senior SBA loan becomes:

\$2,275,000 - \$230,000 - \$200,000 = \$1,845,000

Assume that lowers the monthly payment again to approximately \$16,850. Annual debt service is now:

\$16,850 x 12 = \$202,200 annual debt service

Revised DSCR becomes:

$275,000 / $202,200 = 1.36 DSCR

Now the lender sees an even stronger coverage ratio. Daniel still has roughly $30,000 of personal liquidity after his equity injection, and the business will have $50,000 of loan-funded working capital plus $25,000 retained from Daniel's remaining funds placed into operations. Total practical operating cushion at closing remains:

$50,000 + $25,000 = $75,000 available working capital

Now let us go a step further and evaluate what would have happened if Daniel had ignored structuring and simply used more cash instead of seller financing. Suppose he had decided to increase his injection by $100,000 from family funds to reduce the loan without bringing in seller carry. That would mean:

Revised borrower injection = $330,000 Project cost = $2,275,000 Senior loan = $2,275,000 - $330,000 = $1,945,000

Assume the payment on $1,945,000 is around $17,750 monthly. Annual debt service would be:

$17,750 x 12 = $213,000 annual debt service

DSCR would then be:

$275,000 / $213,000 = 1.29 DSCR

That is still acceptable, but not as strong as the seller-carry structure. More importantly, Daniel would have had to come up with an extra $100,000 in true cash, which might leave the overall liquidity picture weaker or harder to document. So even though a bigger borrower injection can help, it is not always the best answer. In this case, the seller note produces a stronger DSCR and a more elegant capital structure with less strain on the borrower.

Now let us examine the seller's position. The seller note is $200,000. Assume the note accrues simple interest at 6% annually during the 24-month standby period, with no payments due during that time. At the end of two years, the accrued interest would be:

$200,000 x 0.06 = $12,000 per year $12,000 x 2 = $24,000 accrued over two years

Balance due after standby if accrued and unpaid would be:

$200,000 + $24,000 = $224,000

If that balance then amortizes over 10 years at 6%, the monthly payment would be roughly $2,487. By that time, however, Daniel expects business performance to improve under his ownership. Suppose revenue and efficiency improvements increase adjusted annual cash flow from $275,000 to $335,000 by year three. The senior SBA debt remains $202,200 annually, and now the seller note begins requiring about:

$2,487 x 12 = $29,844 annual seller-note debt service

Total annual debt service beginning in year three would be:

$202,200 + $29,844 = $232,044

Revised future DSCR after business improvement becomes:

$335,000 / $232,044 = 1.44 DSCR

This is a crucial insight. By placing the seller note on standby, Daniel avoids pressure during the transition period when the risk is highest. By the time the seller payments begin, improved operations are expected to support the extra debt. That is precisely how layered capital should work. It shifts payment pressure away from the most fragile phase of the deal and into a period when cash flow is likely stronger.

Let us also consider lender psychology numerically. The lender initially faced a 90% leverage position on a $2,300,000 project, with borderline DSCR and weak liquidity. After restructuring, the lender now sees:

Total project cost: $2,275,000 Borrower equity: $230,000 Seller standby support: $200,000 Senior loan: $1,845,000

From the lender's perspective, the total non-senior support in the transaction is:

$230,000 + $200,000 = $430,000

Now the senior lender's effective funded percentage of the total project becomes:

$1,845,000 / $2,275,000 = 81.1%

That is far more attractive than the original structure, where the senior lender would have been at:

$2,070,000 / $2,300,000 = 90.0%

This means the lender's effective position improved from 90.0% of cost to 81.1% of cost due to the layered capital design. That is a major reduction in exposure. Even if the seller note does not function exactly like equity in every context, it still adds meaningful structural support and lowers risk perception.

Now let us summarize the before-and-after comparison.

Original structure Project cost: $2,300,000 Borrower injection: $230,000 Seller financing: $0 Senior SBA loan: $2,070,000 Annual debt service: $226,800 Adjusted cash flow: $275,000 DSCR: 1.21 Post-close liquidity: weak

Restructured layered-capital deal Project cost: $2,275,000 Borrower injection: $230,000 Seller full-standby note: $200,000 Senior SBA loan: $1,845,000 Annual debt service: $202,200 Adjusted cash flow: $275,000 DSCR: 1.36 Post-close liquidity: stronger Lender effective funded percentage: 81.1%

This example shows why advanced SBA structuring is about more than plugging numbers into a template. The raw transaction did not change dramatically. Daniel is still buying essentially the same business and the same building. What changed was the design of the capital stack. By adding a standby seller note, preserving practical liquidity, slightly refining the working capital allocation, and reducing senior leverage, the transaction became dramatically stronger.

The lesson is clear. When a deal is close but not quite there, the solution is not always more borrower cash. Sometimes the smarter answer is layered capital. Seller financing can reduce debt service. A thoughtful equity injection can satisfy commitment requirements without draining reserves. Properly allocated working capital can protect the business after closing. And when these pieces are coordinated, the lender sees not just a transaction, but a well-engineered structure designed for approval and performance. That is the essence of advanced SBA commercial mortgage loan structuring.

Chapter 7

Lender Selection, Deal Positioning, and Strategic Submission for SBA Commercial Mortgage Approval

At the advanced level of SBA commercial mortgage loan structuring, one of the most overlooked yet powerful factors in getting deals approved is lender selection and deal positioning. Many borrowers and even experienced loan professionals assume that if a deal meets SBA guidelines, it should be approved by any SBA lender. In reality, this is far from true. Every lender has its own credit culture, risk tolerance, preferred industries, geographic focus, and internal overlays that go beyond SBA minimum standards. A deal that is declined by one lender can be quickly approved by another—not because the deal changed, but because the lender was a better fit. Mastering lender selection is one of the fastest ways to increase approval rates and close more complex transactions.

The first concept to understand is that SBA guidelines provide a framework, not a guarantee. Lenders interpret these guidelines differently based on their own risk appetite. Some lenders are aggressive and comfortable with tighter debt service coverage ratios, startup businesses, or borrowers with limited experience. Others are conservative and prefer strong cash flow, experienced operators, and low-risk industries. Advanced structuring involves identifying the type of deal you have and matching it with a lender that is naturally inclined to approve it.

Deal positioning begins long before submission. It starts with analyzing the strengths and weaknesses of the transaction and determining how to present it in the most favorable light. Every deal has both positive and negative aspects. The goal is not to hide weaknesses, but to frame them in a way that is understandable and mitigated. For example, if a borrower lacks direct industry experience, the deal can be positioned around transferable skills, strong management support, or a detailed transition plan with the seller. If cash flow is slightly below ideal thresholds, the structure can emphasize compensating factors such as liquidity, collateral, or growth potential.

One of the most important elements of deal positioning is the executive summary. This is often the first document a lender reviews, and it sets the tone for the entire file. A strong executive summary clearly explains the borrower, the business, the property, the loan request, and the key strengths of the deal. It should answer the lender's primary questions before they are even asked. Advanced structuring involves crafting this summary in a way that highlights the deal's strengths while addressing potential concerns proactively.

Understanding lender overlays is critical in advanced structuring. Overlays are additional requirements imposed by lenders beyond SBA guidelines. These may include higher minimum DSCR thresholds, stricter credit requirements, limitations on certain industries, or preferences for specific deal types. By understanding these overlays, you can avoid submitting deals to lenders that are unlikely to approve them. This not only saves time but also protects the borrower from unnecessary credit inquiries and delays.

Another key factor is relationship management. Experienced loan professionals often develop relationships with multiple SBA lenders, allowing them to understand each lender's preferences and decision-making process. These relationships can provide valuable insights into which lenders are currently active in certain markets or open to specific types of deals. Advanced structuring involves leveraging these relationships to position deals effectively and select the best possible lending partner.

Timing also plays a role in lender selection. Lenders' appetites can change based on market conditions, internal capacity, and portfolio performance. A lender that was aggressive six months ago may become more conservative, while another may be actively seeking to grow its SBA portfolio. Advanced structuring involves staying informed about these changes and adjusting lender selection strategies accordingly.

Another important concept is pre-screening deals before formal submission. Instead of submitting a full application immediately, advanced loan professionals often present a summary of the deal to multiple lenders to gauge interest. This allows them to identify the most receptive lender before committing to a full underwriting process. Pre-screening reduces wasted effort and increases efficiency.

Packaging and presentation are critical components of deal positioning. A well-organized file with clear documentation, detailed explanations, and consistent information is far more likely to be approved than a disorganized one. Advanced structuring involves presenting the deal in a way that makes it easy for underwriters to understand and approve. This includes providing clear financial summaries, supporting documentation for all assumptions, and a logical flow of information.

Another advanced strategy is tailoring the deal to the lender. While the core structure of the deal remains the same, certain elements can be emphasized or adjusted based on the lender's preferences. For example, a lender that prioritizes cash flow may respond well to detailed financial analysis, while a lender focused on collateral may place more weight on property value and equity. Understanding these preferences allows you to position the deal more effectively.

Communication is also a key factor in successful deal positioning. Maintaining open and proactive communication with the lender throughout the process helps build trust and address issues quickly. Advanced structuring involves anticipating questions, providing timely responses, and ensuring that the lender has all the information needed to move forward.

Reputation and credibility play a significant role in lender decisions. Borrowers and loan professionals who consistently present well-structured deals and accurate information build a reputation that can positively influence future transactions. Advanced structuring involves maintaining high standards of professionalism and accuracy in every deal.

Another important concept is managing expectations. Not every deal will be approved, and understanding the likelihood of approval before submission is crucial. Advanced structuring involves being realistic about the strengths and weaknesses of a deal and setting appropriate expectations with borrowers. This helps avoid frustration and ensures that efforts are focused on viable opportunities.

As you gain experience, you will begin to see patterns in lender behavior and deal outcomes. You will develop an intuitive sense of which deals are likely to be approved and which require additional structuring. This insight allows you to refine your approach and improve your success rate over time.

Ultimately, lender selection and deal positioning are about alignment. It is about aligning the deal with the right lender, the right presentation, and the right strategy. When these elements come together, even complex transactions can be approved efficiently and successfully.

Real-Life Math Example: Lender Selection Impact on SBA Loan Approval and Structuring

To understand the impact of lender selection and deal positioning, let's walk through a real-world example where the same deal produces different outcomes depending on how it is structured and which lender is chosen.

Consider a borrower named Carlos who is purchasing a commercial property and business for $2,000,000. He plans to put down 10%, or $200,000, resulting in a loan amount of $1,800,000. The estimated monthly payment is $16,500.

Annual debt service:

$16,500 × 12 = $198,000

The business generates adjusted net income of $240,000. Initial DSCR:

$240,000 ÷ $198,000 ≈ 1.21

This is slightly below the 1.25 threshold preferred by many lenders.

Carlos submits the deal to Lender A, which has a strict DSCR requirement of 1.25. Based on their guidelines, the deal is declined.

Now we explore how structuring and lender selection can change the outcome.

Step 1: Adjust Loan Structure Carlos increases his down payment by $50,000, bringing total equity to $250,000. The new loan amount is $1,750,000.

New monthly payment: $16,000 Annual debt service:

$16,000 × 12 = $192,000

Revised DSCR:

$240,000 ÷ $192,000 ≈ 1.25

Now the deal meets the minimum requirement.

Step 2: Introduce Seller Note The seller agrees to carry a $150,000 note on standby, reducing the SBA loan to $1,600,000.

New monthly payment: $14,600 Annual debt service:

$14,600 × 12 = $175,200

Revised DSCR:

$240,000 ÷ $175,200 ≈ 1.37

Step 3: Compare Lender Outcomes

Lender A (strict): Requires DSCR ≥ 1.25 → Approves after restructuring Lender B (flexible): Accepts DSCR ≥ 1.20 → Would have approved original deal Lender C (aggressive): Accepts DSCR ≥ 1.15 with compensating factors → Approves immediately

Step 4: Evaluate Total Cost Impact

Original structure:

Loan: $1,800,000 Annual debt service: $198,000

Restructured deal:

Loan: $1,600,000 Annual debt service: $175,200

Annual savings:

$198,000 – $175,200 = $22,800

Over 10 years:

$22,800 × 10 = $228,000

This demonstrates that structuring not only improves approval chances but also significantly reduces long-term costs.

Step 5: Final Outcome

By selecting the right lender and restructuring the deal, Carlos achieves:

Higher DSCR: 1.37 Lower loan amount: $1,600,000 Reduced annual payments: $175,200 Improved approval probability

This example highlights a critical lesson: the same deal can produce vastly different outcomes depending on lender selection and structuring strategy. Choosing the right lender and positioning the deal effectively can be the difference between denial and approval, as well as significantly impact long-term financial performance.

Chapter 8

Structuring Complex SBA Deals with Multiple Businesses, Mixed-Use Properties, and Layered Income Streams

As you move deeper into advanced SBA commercial mortgage loan structuring, you begin to encounter deals that go far beyond simple single-business, single-property transactions. These are the types of opportunities that often produce the highest returns—but also require the highest level of skill to structure correctly. Complex SBA deals may involve multiple businesses under one ownership group, mixed-use properties with both commercial and residential components, or layered income streams that must be carefully analyzed and presented. This chapter focuses on how to structure these advanced scenarios in a way that aligns with SBA guidelines while maximizing approval probability and long-term profitability.

The first concept to understand is that complexity does not automatically mean risk—unless it is poorly structured. In fact, many complex deals are inherently strong because they involve diversified income, multiple revenue sources, and asset-backed operations. However, lenders tend to approach complexity cautiously because it increases the likelihood of misinterpretation or hidden risk. Advanced structuring is about taking that complexity and organizing it into a clear, logical, and easily understandable format that reduces confusion and builds confidence.

One of the most common complex scenarios involves multiple businesses operating under a single borrower or ownership group. For example, a borrower may own a primary operating business along with additional related or unrelated businesses. SBA guidelines allow for the inclusion of affiliated businesses in certain situations, but the way these businesses are structured and presented is critical. Advanced structuring involves determining whether these businesses should be combined for cash flow purposes, separated to reduce risk, or selectively included to strengthen the overall profile.

When multiple businesses are involved, the concept of global cash flow becomes essential. Instead of evaluating each business in isolation, lenders may look at the combined financial performance of all affiliated entities. This can be advantageous when one business is stronger than another, as it allows the stronger entity to support the overall deal. However, it also introduces complexity, as all businesses must be documented, analyzed, and aligned with SBA affiliation rules. Advanced structuring involves deciding when global cash flow strengthens the deal and when it may introduce unnecessary complications.

Mixed-use properties present another layer of complexity. These properties may include a combination of commercial and residential units, such as a building with retail space on the ground floor and apartments above. SBA guidelines typically require that a majority of the property be owner-occupied for eligibility. Advanced structuring involves ensuring that the property meets these requirements while also maximizing the value of any additional income streams generated by non-owner-occupied portions.

Rental income from mixed-use properties can be a powerful addition to cash flow, but it must be handled carefully. Lenders will evaluate the stability and reliability of rental income, often applying discounts or requiring historical documentation. Advanced structuring involves presenting rental income in a way that is both conservative and supportive of the deal. This may include providing lease agreements, rent rolls, and market data to validate income projections.

Another advanced scenario involves layered income streams within a single business. For example, a business may generate revenue from multiple sources such as product sales, service contracts, subscriptions, and ancillary services. Each of these income streams may have different levels of stability and predictability. Advanced structuring involves analyzing these streams individually and collectively, highlighting the most stable components while addressing any variability.

Seasonality is another factor that can complicate income analysis. Some businesses experience significant fluctuations in revenue throughout the year. Advanced structuring involves normalizing this income to reflect a realistic annual performance while also explaining seasonal trends to lenders. This ensures that the business is evaluated fairly and accurately.

When dealing with complex income structures, clarity becomes even more important. Lenders must be able to understand how each component contributes to the overall financial picture. Advanced structuring involves breaking down income streams into clear categories, providing detailed explanations, and supporting all claims with documentation. This reduces confusion and builds confidence in the deal.

Another important consideration is risk distribution. In complex deals, risk may be spread across multiple entities, properties, or income sources. Advanced structuring involves identifying where risks exist and ensuring that they are balanced by strengths elsewhere in the deal. For example, a property with variable rental income may be supported by a stable operating business, creating an overall balanced risk profile.

Ownership and entity structure also become more critical in complex deals. Multiple businesses and properties may require multiple entities, each with its own ownership and operational structure. Advanced structuring involves organizing these entities in a way that is both compliant and efficient. This includes clearly defining relationships between entities and ensuring that all documentation aligns with SBA requirements.

Lender selection becomes even more important in complex transactions. Not all lenders are comfortable with multi-entity or mixed-use deals. Advanced structuring involves identifying lenders with experience and appetite for these types of transactions. This increases the likelihood of approval and reduces the risk of delays or misunderstandings.

Another key strategy is simplifying complexity wherever possible. While some deals are inherently complex, unnecessary complications should be avoided. Advanced structuring involves streamlining the deal, removing redundant elements, and focusing on the core components that drive value. The goal is to make the deal as straightforward as possible without sacrificing its strengths. Documentation and presentation are critical in complex deals. Detailed financial statements, clear ownership charts, and comprehensive explanations are essential. Advanced structuring involves creating a package that allows the lender to quickly understand the deal, even if it involves multiple moving parts. This level of organization can significantly improve approval chances.

As you gain experience, you will begin to see complex deals as opportunities rather than challenges. These transactions often offer higher returns and greater flexibility, but they require a higher level of expertise to structure effectively. By mastering these techniques, you position yourself to handle some of the most profitable opportunities in SBA commercial mortgage lending.

Ultimately, structuring complex deals is about clarity, balance, and strategy. It is about taking multiple components and aligning them into a cohesive, approvable transaction. When done correctly, even the most complex deals can be presented in a way that feels simple and compelling to lenders.

Real-Life Math Example: Structuring a Multi-Business and Mixed-Use SBA Deal

In this example, we will walk through a complex SBA transaction involving multiple businesses and a mixed-use property, demonstrating how advanced structuring can improve approval and financial performance.

Consider a borrower named Elena who owns two businesses: a restaurant and a catering company. She is purchasing a mixed-use property for $2,400,000 that includes a restaurant space and four residential rental units.

Breakdown:

Property purchase: $2,400,000 Restaurant income (annual): $300,000 gross revenue, $120,000 net Catering business income (annual): $200,000 gross revenue, $80,000 net Rental income: $2,000 per unit × 4 units × 12 months = $96,000

Total initial net income:

Restaurant: $120,000 Catering: $80,000 Rental: $96,000

Total: $296,000

Elena plans a 10% down payment of $240,000, resulting in a loan amount of $2,160,000. The monthly payment is approximately $19,800.

Annual debt service:

$19,800 × 12 = $237,600

Initial DSCR:

$296,000 ÷ $237,600 ≈ 1.25

At first glance, the deal meets minimum requirements. However, lenders may discount rental income or view the catering business as less stable.

Now we apply advanced structuring.

Step 1: Apply Rental Income Discount Assume lender applies a 25% vacancy/expense factor:

$96,000 × 0.75 = $72,000 adjusted rental income

Revised total income:

$120,000 + $80,000 + $72,000 = $272,000

Revised DSCR:

$272,000 ÷ $237,600 ≈ 1.14

Now the deal appears weak.

Step 2: Combine Global Cash Flow Elena also owns a small consulting business generating $40,000 net income. Including this:

$272,000 + $40,000 = $312,000

New DSCR:

$312,000 ÷ $237,600 ≈ 1.31

Step 3: Introduce Seller Note Seller carries $200,000 on standby, reducing loan to $1,960,000.

New monthly payment: $18,000 Annual debt service:

$18,000 × 12 = $216,000

Revised DSCR:

$312,000 ÷ $216,000 ≈ 1.44

Step 4: Revenue Growth Adjustment Elena plans to expand catering operations, increasing net income by $30,000.

New total income:

$312,000 + $30,000 = $342,000

Final DSCR:

$342,000 ÷ $216,000 ≈ 1.58

Step 5: Final Structure Summary

Loan amount: $1,960,000 Annual income: $342,000 Annual debt service: $216,000 Final DSCR: 1.58

This example shows how a complex deal can initially appear marginal but become strong through advanced structuring. By combining income streams, adjusting rental assumptions, introducing a seller note, and incorporating growth projections, the deal transforms into a highly attractive transaction.

The key takeaway is that complexity can be an advantage when structured correctly. Multiple income streams and diversified operations can strengthen a deal, but only if they are presented clearly and strategically. Mastering this skill allows you to unlock higher-level opportunities in SBA commercial mortgage lending.

Chapter 9

Advanced Loan Structuring Using SBA 7(a) vs. 504—Strategic Decision Making and Hybrid Approaches

At the highest level of SBA commercial mortgage loan structuring, one of the most powerful decisions you can make is selecting the right loan program—or combining elements strategically—to optimize both approval and long-term financial performance. The two primary SBA programs used in commercial real estate and business financing are the SBA 7(a) and the SBA 504 loan programs. While most borrowers are introduced to these programs at a basic level, advanced structuring requires a deep understanding of how to strategically choose between them, when to use one over the other, and how to design deals that maximize the strengths of each.

The SBA 7(a) loan program is known for its flexibility. It allows for a wide range of uses including business acquisition, real estate purchase, refinancing, working capital, equipment, and more. This flexibility makes it ideal for complex transactions where multiple uses of proceeds must be combined into a single loan. However, this flexibility often comes at the cost of higher interest rates and fully amortizing debt structures that can result in higher monthly payments.

On the other hand, the SBA 504 loan program is designed specifically for real estate and large fixed assets. It typically involves a structure with a bank providing 50% of the financing, a Certified Development Company (CDC) providing 40%, and the borrower contributing 10%. One of the biggest advantages of the 504 program is the long-term fixed interest rate on the CDC portion, which can provide stability and lower overall financing costs. However, the 504 program is less flexible than the 7(a), as it cannot be used for business acquisitions or working capital.

Advanced structuring begins with understanding the trade-offs between these two programs. The decision is not simply about which program is available, but which one creates the best overall outcome for the borrower. This includes evaluating factors such as cash flow, interest rates, loan terms, use of proceeds, and long-term financial goals.

One of the most important considerations is debt service. The structure of the loan directly impacts monthly payments and, therefore, the debt service coverage ratio. The SBA 504 program often results in lower monthly payments due to its longer amortization and fixed-rate structure, particularly on the CDC portion. This can improve DSCR and make deals more approvable. However, the 7(a) program may still be preferable in cases where flexibility is needed, even if it results in higher payments.

Another key factor is the use of proceeds. If a transaction involves multiple components such as business acquisition, working capital, and real estate, the 7(a) program may be the only viable option. However, advanced structuring may involve separating components of the deal to take advantage of both programs where possible. For example, a borrower may use a 504 loan for the real estate portion and separate financing for the business acquisition. This type of hybrid approach requires careful planning and coordination but can result in significant financial benefits.

Interest rate structure is another critical consideration. The 504 program offers fixed rates on the CDC portion, providing long-term stability and protection against rising interest rates. The 7(a) program typically involves variable rates, which may be lower initially but can increase over time. Advanced structuring involves evaluating market conditions and the borrower's risk tolerance to determine which structure is more appropriate.

Prepayment penalties and flexibility also play a role in decision-making. The 504 program often includes prepayment penalties on the CDC portion, which may limit flexibility if the borrower plans to refinance or sell the property in the near future. The 7(a) program may offer more flexibility in this regard, depending on the structure. Advanced structuring involves aligning the loan terms with the borrower's long-term plans.

Another important consideration is the borrower's growth strategy. For borrowers planning to expand rapidly or acquire additional properties, the flexibility of the 7(a) program may be more advantageous. For those seeking long-term stability and predictable payments, the 504 program may be a better fit. Advanced structuring involves aligning the loan program with the borrower's strategic goals.

Collateral and equity requirements also differ between the programs. The 504 program typically requires a lower equity injection for established businesses, which can preserve borrower liquidity. The 7(a) program may require higher equity in certain scenarios, particularly for startups or higher-risk transactions. Understanding these differences allows for more effective structuring.

Another advanced strategy involves timing. In some cases, a borrower may initially use a 7(a) loan for flexibility and later refinance into a 504 loan for lower long-term costs. This approach allows the borrower to take advantage of the strengths of both programs at different stages of the business lifecycle. However, this requires careful planning and consideration of costs and timing.

Lender preferences also play a role in program selection. Some lenders specialize in 7(a) loans, while others focus on 504 transactions. Advanced structuring involves selecting lenders that are well-suited to the chosen program and have experience with similar deals.

As deals become more complex, the ability to evaluate and compare different loan structures becomes increasingly important. Advanced structuring involves running multiple scenarios, analyzing the impact of each option, and selecting the one that provides the best overall outcome. This requires not only financial analysis but also a deep understanding of SBA guidelines and lender behavior.

Ultimately, the choice between SBA 7(a) and 504 is not a simple one. It requires a strategic approach that considers all aspects of the deal. By mastering these concepts, you can structure transactions that maximize approval chances, optimize cash flow, and support long-term success.

Real-Life Math Example: Comparing SBA 7(a) vs. 504 Loan Structures

In this example, we will compare two different loan structures for the same transaction to demonstrate how program selection impacts cash flow, DSCR, and long-term costs.

Consider a borrower named Kevin who is purchasing a commercial property for $2,000,000. The business generates adjusted net income of $260,000 annually.

Option 1: SBA 7(a) Loan

Loan amount: $1,800,000 (10% down payment of $200,000) Interest rate: 10% Term: 25 years

Monthly payment: approximately $16,500

Annual debt service:

$16,500 × 12 = $198,000

DSCR:

$260,000 ÷ $198,000 ≈ 1.31

Option 2: SBA 504 Loan

Structure:

Bank loan (50%): $1,000,000 CDC loan (40%): $800,000 Borrower equity (10%): $200,000

Bank loan terms: Interest rate: 8% Term: 25 years Monthly payment: approximately $7,700

CDC loan terms: Interest rate: 6% (fixed) Term: 25 years Monthly payment: approximately $5,150

Total monthly payment:

$7,700 + $5,150 = $12,850

Annual debt service:

$12,850 × 12 = $154,200

DSCR:

$260,000 ÷ $154,200 ≈ 1.69

Comparison Summary

SBA 7(a):

Loan: $1,800,000 Annual debt service: $198,000 DSCR: 1.31

SBA 504:

Loan structure: $1,000,000 + $800,000 Annual debt service: $154,200 DSCR: 1.69

Annual payment difference:

$198,000 – $154,200 = $43,800

Over 10 years:

$43,800 × 10 = $438,000

Advanced Structuring Insight

While the 504 loan provides significantly lower payments and higher DSCR, it lacks flexibility. If Kevin needed additional funds for working capital or business acquisition, the 7(a) loan might still be necessary.

Now consider a hybrid approach:

Kevin uses a 504 loan for the real estate and secures separate financing for $200,000 in working capital.

This allows him to benefit from lower real estate payments while still accessing needed funds.

Final Outcome

By choosing the right loan structure, Kevin achieves:

Lower monthly payments Higher DSCR Improved approval likelihood Significant long-term savings

This example highlights the importance of strategic decision-making in SBA loan structuring. The choice between 7(a) and 504—or a combination of both—can dramatically impact both approval and financial performance.

Chapter 10

Exit Strategy, Refinancing, and Long-Term Wealth Structuring with SBA Commercial Mortgage Loans

At the most advanced level of SBA commercial mortgage loan structuring, success is no longer defined by simply getting a deal approved. True mastery comes from designing a transaction that performs not just at closing, but over years and even decades. This requires thinking beyond the initial loan and focusing on exit strategy, refinancing opportunities, equity growth, and long-term wealth creation. The most sophisticated borrowers and loan professionals structure deals with the end in mind, understanding that every decision made at origination will influence future flexibility, profitability, and scalability.

The concept of exit strategy begins with a simple but powerful question: what is the long-term plan for this asset or business? Some borrowers intend to hold properties and businesses indefinitely, building wealth through cash flow and appreciation. Others plan to refinance after a few years to reduce costs or extract equity. Some may eventually sell the asset at a profit. Advanced structuring involves aligning the initial loan with these future goals, ensuring that the borrower is not locked into a structure that limits their options.

Refinancing is one of the most common and powerful exit strategies in SBA lending. Over time, businesses grow, property values increase, and market conditions change. A borrower who initially qualified for an SBA loan with higher interest rates or tighter cash flow may later be eligible for conventional financing with better terms. Advanced structuring involves positioning the borrower to take advantage of these opportunities. This includes maintaining strong financial performance, improving credit, and building equity.

Equity growth is a central component of long-term wealth creation. As loan balances are paid down and property values increase, borrowers build equity in their assets. Advanced structuring involves maximizing this growth by selecting properties with strong appreciation potential and structuring loans in a way that supports long-term value creation. This may include choosing fixed-rate financing for stability or structuring deals that allow for future expansion and improvements.

Cash flow management is equally important. While equity builds over time, cash flow provides immediate financial benefits and supports ongoing operations. Advanced structuring involves balancing these two elements, ensuring that the borrower has sufficient cash flow to operate and grow while also building long-term wealth. This may involve selecting loan terms that optimize monthly payments or allocating funds toward revenue-generating improvements.

Another key consideration is timing. The timing of a refinance or sale can significantly impact financial outcomes. Refinancing too early may result in unnecessary costs, while waiting too long may mean missing favorable market conditions. Advanced structuring involves monitoring market trends, interest rates, and business performance to determine the optimal timing for these decisions.

Prepayment penalties are an important factor in exit strategy planning. Many SBA loans include prepayment penalties, particularly in the early years. Understanding these penalties and how they decline over time is essential for planning future refinancing or sale. Advanced structuring involves aligning the borrower's timeline with these penalties to minimize costs.

Another advanced strategy is equity extraction. As property values increase and loan balances decrease, borrowers may be able to access their equity through refinancing or lines of credit. This capital can be used to fund additional investments, expand the business, or diversify into new opportunities. Advanced structuring involves planning for these possibilities and ensuring that the borrower is positioned to take advantage of them.

Portfolio growth is a natural extension of successful SBA structuring. Many borrowers use their first SBA loan as a stepping stone to acquire additional properties or businesses. Advanced structuring involves designing deals that support this growth, including maintaining liquidity, building strong financial performance, and establishing relationships with lenders.

Risk management remains a critical component of long-term strategy. While growth and expansion are important, they must be balanced with stability. Advanced structuring involves ensuring that the borrower is not overleveraged and that each deal contributes positively to the overall portfolio. This includes maintaining adequate reserves, diversifying income streams, and monitoring performance.

Another important concept is tax efficiency. Real estate and business ownership offer various tax advantages, including depreciation and expense deductions. Advanced structuring involves coordinating with tax professionals to maximize these benefits while ensuring compliance. While tax strategy is beyond the scope of this book, understanding its impact is essential for long-term planning. Succession planning is also a key consideration for many borrowers. As businesses grow, owners may eventually want to transfer ownership to family members, partners, or buyers. Advanced structuring involves designing deals that facilitate these transitions, including clear ownership structures and flexible financing arrangements.

Documentation and record-keeping are essential for long-term success. Maintaining accurate financial records, tracking performance, and documenting improvements all support future refinancing and valuation. Advanced structuring involves establishing systems that make this process efficient and reliable.

As you move into advanced levels of SBA structuring, you will begin to think not just as a borrower or broker, but as an investor and strategist. Every deal becomes part of a larger plan, contributing to long-term wealth and financial independence. This perspective transforms the way you approach transactions and opens the door to greater opportunities.

Ultimately, the goal of advanced SBA commercial mortgage loan structuring is not just to close deals, but to build a sustainable and scalable financial future. By aligning your initial structure with long-term goals, you position yourself for continued success and growth.

Real-Life Math Example: Long-Term Wealth and Exit Strategy Planning

In this example, we will analyze how a well-structured SBA loan can create long-term wealth through refinancing, equity growth, and strategic planning.

Consider a borrower named Rachel who purchases a commercial property for $1,800,000 using an SBA 7(a) loan.

Initial structure:

Purchase price: $1,800,000 Down payment (10%): $180,000 Loan amount: $1,620,000 Interest rate: 10% Term: 25 years

Monthly payment: approximately $14,800

Annual debt service:

$\$14,800 \times 12 = \$177,600$

The property generates net operating income of $220,000 annually.

Initial DSCR:

$\$220,000 \div \$177,600 \approx 1.24$

Year 1–5 Performance

Rachel improves operations, increasing income by $30,000 annually.

New income:

$220,000 + $30,000 = $250,000

DSCR:

$250,000 ÷ $177,600 ≈ 1.41

During this period, she also pays down the loan balance. After 5 years, the loan balance is approximately $1,450,000.

Property Appreciation

Assume the property appreciates at 4% annually.

Future value after 5 years:

$1,800,000 × (1.04)^5 ≈ $2,190,000

Equity position:

$2,190,000 − $1,450,000 = $740,000

The key takeaway is that every SBA loan should be structured with the future in mind. The decisions made at the beginning of a deal can create opportunities for growth, flexibility, and financial success for years to come.

Chapter 11

Scaling SBA Commercial Mortgage Financing into a Portfolio Strategy and Building a Lending Empire

At the highest level of SBA commercial mortgage loan mastery, the focus shifts from structuring individual deals to building a repeatable, scalable system for acquiring multiple assets and businesses over time. This is where you transition from being a borrower or deal-maker into a portfolio builder and strategic investor. The goal is no longer just to get approved for one loan, but to create a pipeline of opportunities, leverage each deal to unlock the next, and build a long-term engine of income, equity, and financial control. This chapter focuses on how to scale SBA financing into a portfolio strategy and ultimately build a lending and investment ecosystem that compounds over time.

The first principle of scaling is understanding that each SBA loan is not an isolated transaction—it is a stepping stone. Every deal you complete strengthens your financial profile, builds relationships with lenders, and increases your credibility. Over time, this allows you to access larger loans, better terms, and more complex opportunities. Advanced structuring involves designing each deal in a way that supports future growth, including maintaining strong financials, preserving liquidity, and building a track record of successful operations.

Cash flow is the engine that drives scalability. While equity builds long-term wealth, cash flow provides the resources needed to pursue new opportunities. Advanced portfolio structuring involves prioritizing deals that generate strong and stable cash flow, allowing you to reinvest profits into additional acquisitions. This creates a cycle where each property or business contributes to the growth of the overall portfolio.

Leverage is another key component of scaling. SBA loans allow borrowers to acquire assets with relatively low down payments, often around 10%. This means that a relatively small amount of capital can control a much larger asset base. Advanced structuring involves using leverage strategically, ensuring that each deal is strong enough to support its debt while still contributing to overall portfolio growth. Over-leveraging can create risk, but when managed properly, leverage is one of the most powerful tools for building wealth.

One of the most effective scaling strategies is the "acquire, stabilize, and expand" model. In this approach, a borrower acquires a business or property, improves its performance, and then uses the increased cash flow and equity to support additional acquisitions. Advanced structuring involves identifying opportunities where value can be added through operational improvements, cost reductions, or revenue growth. This not only strengthens the current deal but also creates opportunities for future financing.

Another important concept is diversification. A strong portfolio includes a mix of assets and income streams, reducing risk and increasing stability. This may include different types of businesses, properties in various locations, or multiple revenue streams within a single asset. Advanced structuring involves building a portfolio that is resilient to market fluctuations and capable of generating consistent returns.

Entity structuring becomes increasingly important as the portfolio grows. Multiple properties and businesses may require separate entities for liability protection and operational efficiency. Advanced structuring involves organizing these entities in a way that supports scalability while maintaining compliance with SBA guidelines. This may include creating holding companies, separating operating businesses from real estate, and clearly defining ownership structures.

Lender relationships are a critical component of scaling. As you complete more deals, you build trust and credibility with lenders. This can lead to faster approvals, more flexible terms, and access to larger loan amounts. Advanced structuring involves maintaining strong relationships with multiple lenders, allowing you to match each deal with the best possible financing partner.

Another key strategy is reinvestment. Instead of extracting all profits from each deal, advanced portfolio builders reinvest a portion of their earnings into new opportunities. This accelerates growth and allows the portfolio to expand more rapidly. Reinvestment can take many forms, including funding down payments, covering closing costs, or investing in improvements that increase asset value.

Timing is also important in scaling. Not every opportunity should be pursued immediately. Advanced structuring involves evaluating market conditions, interest rates, and business performance to determine the best time to acquire new assets. This strategic approach helps maximize returns and minimize risk.

Risk management becomes increasingly important as the portfolio grows. While expansion is the goal, it must be balanced with stability. Advanced structuring involves ensuring that each deal contributes positively to the overall portfolio and that the borrower is not overextended. This includes maintaining reserves, monitoring performance, and adjusting strategies as needed. Another advanced concept is vertical integration. This involves controlling multiple aspects of the business or investment process, such as acquisition, management, and financing. By integrating these functions, borrowers can increase efficiency, reduce costs, and improve profitability. Advanced structuring involves identifying opportunities to integrate operations and create additional value.

Building a lending ecosystem is another powerful strategy. As your portfolio grows, you may begin to act not only as a borrower but also as a lender or investor. This could involve providing financing to other businesses, partnering on deals, or creating investment funds. Advanced structuring involves leveraging your experience and capital to create new income streams and expand your influence in the market.

Documentation and systems are essential for scaling. Managing multiple deals requires organization, consistency, and efficiency. Advanced structuring involves creating systems for tracking financial performance, managing documentation, and coordinating transactions. This allows you to handle a larger volume of deals without becoming overwhelmed.

As you continue to grow, your mindset will shift from transactional thinking to strategic planning. You will begin to see opportunities not just in individual deals, but in how those deals fit into your overall portfolio. This perspective allows you to make more informed decisions and build a sustainable path to long-term wealth.

Ultimately, scaling SBA commercial mortgage financing into a portfolio strategy is about creating a system that works for you. It is about leveraging each deal to unlock the next, building a network of assets that generate income and equity, and positioning yourself for continued growth. By mastering these concepts, you can transform your approach to SBA lending and create a powerful foundation for financial success.

Real-Life Math Example: Scaling an SBA Portfolio from One Deal to Multiple Assets

To understand how SBA financing can be scaled into a portfolio strategy, let's walk through a real-world example of how a borrower builds multiple assets over time using strategic reinvestment and structuring.

Deal 1: Initial Acquisition

Purchase price: $1,500,000 Down payment (10%): $150,000 Loan amount: $1,350,000 Monthly payment: $12,300

Annual debt service:

$12,300 × 12 = $147,600

Net income from business/property: $200,000

DSCR:

$200,000 ÷ $147,600 ≈ 1.36

Annual cash flow after debt:

$200,000 – $147,600 = $52,400

Year 1–3 Growth

The borrower improves operations, increasing income by $30,000.

New income:

$200,000 + $30,000 = $230,000

New cash flow:

$230,000 – $147,600 = $82,400 annually

Over 3 years:

$82,400 × 3 = $247,200 accumulated cash flow

Deal 2: Second Acquisition

The borrower uses $200,000 from accumulated cash flow as a down payment.

Purchase price: $2,000,000 Down payment: $200,000 Loan amount: $1,800,000 Monthly payment: $16,500

Annual debt service:

$16,500 × 12 = $198,000

Income from second deal: $260,000

DSCR:

$260,000 ÷ $198,000 ≈ 1.31

Cash flow from second deal:

$260,000 − $198,000 = $62,000

Combined Portfolio Performance

Total income:

$230,000 + $260,000 = $490,000

Total debt service:

$147,600 + $198,000 = $345,600

Combined DSCR:

$490,000 ÷ $345,600 ≈ 1.42

Total annual cash flow:

$82,400 + $62,000 = $144,400

Year 4–6 Growth and Reinvestment

Over 3 years:

$144,400 × 3 = $433,200

The borrower uses $300,000 for a third acquisition.

Deal 3: Third Acquisition

Purchase price: $2,500,000 Down payment: $300,000 Loan amount: $2,200,000 Monthly payment: $20,000

Annual debt service:

$20,000 × 12 = $240,000

Income from third deal: $320,000

DSCR:

$320,000 ÷ $240,000 ≈ 1.33

Cash flow:

$320,000 – $240,000 = $80,000

Final Portfolio Summary

Total income:

$230,000 + $260,000 + $320,000 = $810,000

Total debt service:

$147,600 + $198,000 + $240,000 = $585,600

Combined DSCR:

$810,000 ÷ $585,600 ≈ 1.38

Total annual cash flow:

$82,400 + $62,000 + $80,000 = $224,400

Long-Term Impact

Within 6 years, the borrower has:

Acquired 3 assets Built over $800,000 in annual income Generated over $200,000 in annual cash flow Maintained strong DSCR across the portfolio

This example demonstrates how SBA financing can be used as a foundation for scaling. By reinvesting cash flow, maintaining strong structures, and strategically acquiring new assets, a borrower can build a powerful and sustainable portfolio.

The key takeaway is that each deal is a stepping stone. With the right strategy, SBA loans can be used not just to acquire assets, but to create a long-term system of growth, income, and wealth.

Chapter 12

The Complete Advanced SBA Deal Blueprint—From Opportunity to Approval to Long-Term Wealth

At the highest level of SBA commercial mortgage loan structuring, everything comes together into a single, repeatable system. This final chapter is about mastering the full blueprint—from identifying the right opportunity, to structuring the deal for approval, to executing with precision, and ultimately turning that deal into long-term wealth. By now, you understand cash flow, ownership, lender psychology, capital stacking, program selection, and portfolio scaling. The next step is integrating all of these elements into one cohesive strategy that you can apply over and over again.

The most successful SBA borrowers and deal architects do not approach each transaction randomly. They follow a process. That process begins with opportunity selection. Not every deal is worth pursuing, and advanced structuring starts by identifying opportunities that have the potential to work from both a financial and structural perspective. This includes evaluating purchase price, cash flow, industry stability, property quality, and growth potential. A strong deal at the beginning reduces the amount of structuring required later and increases the likelihood of approval.

Once a potential deal is identified, the next step is initial feasibility analysis. This involves running quick calculations to determine whether the deal is likely to meet basic SBA requirements. This includes estimating debt service, calculating preliminary DSCR, and identifying any obvious red flags. Advanced structuring involves doing this analysis early, before significant time and resources are invested. If a deal does not meet minimum thresholds, adjustments can be made at this stage or the opportunity can be reconsidered.

The next phase is structural design. This is where the deal is shaped to fit within SBA guidelines while maximizing strength. This includes determining the optimal loan program, structuring ownership and entities, designing the capital stack, and allocating use of proceeds. At this stage, every component of the deal is intentionally aligned. Advanced structuring involves considering multiple scenarios and selecting the one that provides the best balance of approval probability, cash flow, and long-term value.

Capital stack design is one of the most critical elements of this phase. As discussed in previous chapters, this involves combining borrower equity, seller financing, and SBA debt in a way that reduces risk and improves financial performance. The goal is not just to meet minimum requirements, but to create a structure that is strong, flexible, and sustainable. This often involves using seller notes, preserving liquidity, and ensuring that the borrower is not overextended.

Cash flow optimization is another key component of the blueprint. This includes analyzing financials, applying add-backs, normalizing income, and structuring debt in a way that supports strong DSCR. Advanced structuring involves presenting cash flow in a way that accurately reflects the business's true performance while addressing any potential concerns. This is where many deals are won or lost.

Once the structure is designed, the next step is deal positioning and packaging. This involves preparing the documentation and narrative that will be presented to the lender. A strong package includes an executive summary, detailed financial analysis, clear ownership structure, and supporting documentation for all assumptions. Advanced structuring involves presenting the deal in a way that is easy to understand and compelling to approve.

Lender selection is the next critical step. As discussed in previous chapters, not all lenders are the same. Advanced structuring involves selecting a lender whose preferences align with the deal. This increases the likelihood of approval and reduces the risk of delays or complications. Pre-screening the deal with potential lenders can also be an effective strategy.

Submission and underwriting are where the structure is tested. During this phase, lenders will review the deal in detail, ask questions, and request additional information. Advanced structuring involves anticipating these questions and addressing them proactively. This includes providing clear explanations, supporting documentation, and timely responses. The goal is to make the underwriting process as smooth as possible.

Closing the deal is not the end of the process—it is the beginning of the next phase. Once the loan is funded, the focus shifts to execution and performance. This includes implementing the business plan, managing operations, and monitoring financial performance. Advanced structuring involves ensuring that the borrower is prepared for this phase and has the resources needed to succeed.

Post-closing strategy is where long-term wealth is created. This includes managing cash flow, building equity, and planning for future opportunities. Advanced structuring involves thinking ahead, identifying potential refinancing opportunities, and positioning the borrower for growth. This may include improving financial performance, increasing property value, or preparing for additional acquisitions.

Another important aspect of the blueprint is continuous improvement. Each deal provides valuable insights that can be applied to future transactions. Advanced structuring involves analyzing outcomes, identifying areas for improvement, and refining strategies over time. This iterative process leads to greater efficiency and success.

Risk management remains a constant throughout the process. Even well-structured deals can encounter challenges, and advanced structuring involves preparing for these scenarios. This includes maintaining reserves, monitoring performance, and adjusting strategies as needed. A proactive approach to risk management ensures long-term stability.

The ultimate goal of this blueprint is to create a repeatable system. By following a structured process, you can approach each deal with confidence and consistency. This not only improves approval rates but also allows you to scale your efforts and build a larger portfolio.

As you reach the end of this series, it is important to recognize that mastery is not a destination but a continuous journey. The principles and strategies outlined in this book provide a strong foundation, but real-world application and experience will further refine your skills. Each deal you complete will deepen your understanding and expand your capabilities.

You are now equipped with the knowledge and tools to structure advanced SBA commercial mortgage transactions at a professional level. Whether you are a borrower, broker, or investor, you have the ability to identify opportunities, design strong deals, and execute with precision. This is the foundation of long-term success in SBA lending and commercial real estate.

The final takeaway is simple but powerful: every deal is an opportunity to build something greater. By applying the advanced structuring principles in this series, you can transform individual transactions into a system of growth, income, and wealth that continues to expand over time.

Real-Life Math Example: The Complete SBA Deal Blueprint in Action

To bring everything together, let's walk through a comprehensive real-world example that demonstrates the full SBA deal blueprint from start to finish.

Step 1: Opportunity Identification

Purchase price (business + real estate): $2,200,000 Projected net income: $260,000

Step 2: Initial Feasibility

Estimated loan (10% down):

Loan amount: $1,980,000 Monthly payment: $18,000

Annual debt service:

$\$18{,}000 \times 12 = \$216{,}000$

Initial DSCR:

$\$260{,}000 \div \$216{,}000 \approx 1.20$

Below target → requires structuring.

Step 3: Capital Stack Design

Introduce:

Borrower equity: $220,000 Seller note (standby): $200,000

New loan amount:

$\$2{,}200{,}000 - \$220{,}000 - \$200{,}000 = \$1{,}780{,}000$

New monthly payment: $16,200

Annual debt service:

$\$16{,}200 \times 12 = \$194{,}400$

Revised DSCR:

$260,000 ÷ $194,400 ≈ 1.34

Step 4: Cash Flow Optimization

Add-backs identified:

Depreciation: $25,000 One-time expenses: $15,000

Adjusted income:

$260,000 + $25,000 + $15,000 = $300,000

New DSCR:

$300,000 ÷ $194,400 ≈ 1.54

Step 5: Final Structuring

Loan amount: $1,780,000 Annual debt service: $194,400 Adjusted income: $300,000 Final DSCR: 1.54

Step 6: 5-Year Performance

Income grows by $40,000:

$300,000 + $40,000 = $340,000

Loan balance after 5 years: ~$1,550,000

Property value grows to $2,600,000

Equity:

$2,600,000 – $1,550,000 = $1,050,000

Step 7: Refinance

New loan at 7%:

Monthly payment: $11,000

Annual debt service:

$11,000 × 12 = $132,000

New DSCR:

$340,000 ÷ $132,000 ≈ 2.58

Annual savings:

$194,400 – $132,000 = $62,400

Step 8: Expansion

Cash-out refinance of $300,000 used for new acquisition.

New total income:

$340,000 + $50,000 = $390,000

New debt service:

$132,000 + $36,000 = $168,000

Combined DSCR:

$390,000 ÷ $168,000 ≈ 2.32

Final Outcome

Through the complete SBA blueprint, the borrower achieves:

Initial approval through structuring Strong DSCR and cash flow Over $1,000,000 in equity Refinancing savings of $62,400 annually Expansion into additional investments

This example demonstrates how advanced SBA structuring is not just about getting deals approved—it is about creating a long-term system for building wealth, scaling investments, and achieving financial independence.

The key takeaway is that when all elements of structuring are combined into a single blueprint, the results can be transformational.

Chapter 13

Advanced SBA Deal Troubleshooting—Fixing Declines, Saving Deals, and Turning Weak Files into Approvals

At the highest level of SBA commercial mortgage loan structuring, one of the most valuable skills you can develop is the ability to troubleshoot and rescue deals that have been declined or appear unworkable. While many loan professionals focus on clean, straightforward transactions, the real opportunity—and often the highest profit—lies in solving complex problems that others cannot. Deals get declined every day for reasons such as low cash flow, weak borrower profiles, insufficient equity, or structural issues. However, a decline is not always the end of the deal. In many cases, it is simply an indication that the deal needs to be restructured. This chapter focuses on how to analyze declined transactions, identify the root causes of the issues, and apply advanced structuring techniques to turn weak files into strong, approvable deals.

The first step in troubleshooting any SBA deal is identifying the true reason for the decline. Lenders may provide general feedback such as "insufficient cash flow" or "high risk," but these explanations often lack specificity. Advanced structuring requires digging deeper to understand exactly what caused the issue. Was the DSCR below the lender's threshold? Was the borrower's credit profile weak? Was there insufficient liquidity or collateral? Was the industry considered high risk? Each of these factors requires a different solution, and understanding the root cause is essential.

Cash flow issues are one of the most common reasons for decline. When DSCR falls below acceptable levels, the deal may appear unapprovable at first glance. However, advanced structuring involves exploring multiple ways to improve cash flow. This may include identifying additional add-backs, normalizing financials, restructuring debt terms, or reducing the loan amount through increased equity or seller financing. In many cases, a combination of these strategies can bring the DSCR above the required threshold.

Borrower profile weaknesses are another common challenge. A borrower with a lower credit score, limited experience, or insufficient liquidity may struggle to secure approval. Advanced structuring involves strengthening the borrower profile through strategic adjustments. This could include adding a co-borrower or partner with stronger credentials, increasing reserves, or providing detailed explanations for any credit issues. The goal is to present a borrower profile that inspires confidence. Equity and capital structure issues also frequently lead to declines. If the borrower does not have sufficient funds for the required down payment or if the capital stack is poorly structured, lenders may view the deal as too risky. Advanced structuring involves redesigning the capital stack to include elements such as seller financing, standby notes, or additional investor contributions. These adjustments can reduce the lender's exposure and improve the overall strength of the deal.

Collateral concerns can also impact approval. While SBA loans are primarily cash flow-driven, collateral still plays a role in risk mitigation. If a deal lacks sufficient collateral, advanced structuring may involve adding additional assets or restructuring the transaction to strengthen the collateral position. This can help offset other weaknesses in the deal.

Industry and business risk are additional factors that lenders consider. Certain industries may be viewed as higher risk due to volatility, regulatory challenges, or market conditions. Advanced structuring involves addressing these concerns through detailed business plans, market analysis, and risk mitigation strategies. Demonstrating stability and growth potential can help overcome industry-related concerns.

Another important aspect of troubleshooting is lender

selection. A deal that is declined by one lender may be approved by another with a different risk tolerance or focus. Advanced structuring involves identifying lenders that are more aligned with the specific characteristics of the deal. This requires knowledge of the lending landscape and an understanding of each lender's preferences.

Deal positioning and presentation also play a critical role in overcoming declines. A poorly presented deal may be misunderstood or undervalued by lenders. Advanced structuring involves re-packaging the deal with clear documentation, detailed explanations, and a compelling narrative. This can significantly improve how the deal is perceived.

Timing can also influence deal outcomes. Market conditions, lender capacity, and business performance can change over time. In some cases, delaying a transaction to strengthen financials or improve conditions may be the best strategy. Advanced structuring involves recognizing when timing is a factor and adjusting accordingly.

Another key concept is incremental improvement. Not all issues need to be solved at once. Sometimes, making a series of small adjustments can gradually strengthen a deal to the point where it becomes approvable. This iterative approach allows for flexibility and creativity in structuring. Communication with lenders is essential during the troubleshooting process. Providing clear explanations, addressing concerns proactively, and maintaining transparency can build trust and improve the likelihood of approval. Advanced structuring involves engaging with lenders as partners in the process rather than adversaries.

Documentation and organization are critical when reworking a declined deal. Lenders need to see that the issues have been addressed and that the new structure is sound. Advanced structuring involves ensuring that all documentation is accurate, complete, and aligned with the revised structure.

As you develop your troubleshooting skills, you will begin to see declines not as failures, but as opportunities. Each declined deal provides valuable insights into lender expectations and structuring strategies. By learning from these experiences, you can improve your approach and increase your success rate.

Ultimately, advanced deal troubleshooting is about problem-solving. It is about identifying obstacles, developing solutions, and creating a structure that works for all parties involved. This skill is one of the most valuable in SBA commercial mortgage lending and can set you apart in a competitive market.

Real-Life Math Example: Turning a Declined SBA Deal into an Approval

In this example, we will walk through a real-world scenario where a declined SBA deal is restructured and successfully approved through advanced troubleshooting techniques.

Initial Scenario (Declined Deal)

Purchase price: $2,100,000 Down payment (10%): $210,000 Loan amount: $1,890,000 Monthly payment: $17,300

Annual debt service:

$17,300 × 12 = $207,600

Business net income: $230,000

Initial DSCR:

$230,000 ÷ $207,600 ≈ 1.11

The deal is declined due to low DSCR and limited liquidity.

Step 1: Identify Add-Backs

Depreciation: $30,000 One-time expenses: $20,000

Adjusted income:

$230,000 + $30,000 + $20,000 = $280,000

Revised DSCR:

$280,000 ÷ $207,600 ≈ 1.35

Now DSCR meets requirements, but liquidity is still an issue.

Step 2: Introduce Seller Financing

Seller agrees to carry $150,000 on standby.

New loan amount:

$2,100,000 – $210,000 – $150,000 = $1,740,000

New monthly payment: $15,900

Annual debt service:

$15,900 × 12 = $190,800

Revised DSCR:

$280,000 ÷ $190,800 ≈ 1.47

Step 3: Improve Liquidity

Borrower retains $75,000 in reserves after closing.

Step 4: Add Co-Borrower

A partner with strong credit and experience is added, strengthening the borrower profile.

Step 5: Lender Selection

The deal is submitted to a lender with experience in similar transactions and a flexible risk profile.

Final Outcome

Loan amount: $1,740,000 Annual debt service: $190,800 Adjusted income: $280,000 Final DSCR: 1.47

The deal is approved.

Comparison Summary

Original DSCR: 1.11 (declined) Final DSCR: 1.47 (approved)

Loan reduced by $150,000 Annual payment reduced by $16,800

Key Takeaway

This example demonstrates that a declined deal is not necessarily a failed deal. By identifying weaknesses, applying strategic adjustments, and selecting the right lender, it is possible to transform a weak transaction into a strong, approvable one.

Mastering this process allows you to unlock opportunities that others overlook and significantly increase your success in SBA commercial mortgage lending.

Chapter 14

Automation, Systems, and AI-Driven SBA Deal Structuring at Scale

At the most advanced level of SBA commercial mortgage loan structuring, success is no longer dependent solely on your ability to analyze and structure individual deals—it is driven by your ability to create systems that consistently generate, evaluate, structure, and close deals at scale. The top performers in this space are not just deal-makers; they are system builders. They leverage automation, technology, and increasingly artificial intelligence to streamline workflows, eliminate inefficiencies, and multiply their output without sacrificing quality. This chapter focuses on how to build a scalable, automated SBA deal structuring system that allows you to handle more deals, faster, with greater precision.

The first step in building a scalable system is understanding that every deal follows a process. From lead generation to closing, each transaction moves through a series of stages: sourcing, qualification, structuring, lender matching, submission, underwriting, and closing. Advanced structuring involves breaking down this process into repeatable steps and identifying which parts can be automated or systematized. This not only increases efficiency but also reduces the likelihood of errors.

Lead generation is the starting point of any scalable system. Without a consistent flow of opportunities, even the best structuring skills will go unused. Advanced systems involve creating multiple lead sources, such as online marketing, referrals, partnerships, and data-driven prospecting. Automation tools can be used to capture and organize leads, ensuring that no opportunity is missed. This creates a steady pipeline of potential deals.

Once leads are generated, the next step is qualification. Not every lead is worth pursuing, and advanced systems use predefined criteria to quickly assess viability. This may include basic financial metrics, credit profiles, and deal parameters. Automation can be used to collect this information through forms, surveys, or integrated systems, allowing for rapid initial analysis. This ensures that time is focused on the most promising opportunities.

Deal structuring is where advanced systems begin to provide significant value. While structuring itself requires expertise, many aspects of the process can be supported by templates, calculators, and AI-driven tools. For example, automated financial models can quickly calculate DSCR, loan amounts, and payment scenarios. AI tools can assist in identifying add-backs, analyzing financial statements, and generating deal summaries. These tools do not replace expertise but enhance it by providing faster and more accurate analysis.

Lender matching is another area where automation can have a major impact. Instead of manually researching lenders for each deal, advanced systems maintain databases of lender preferences, overlays, and deal history. AI can be used to match deals with the most suitable lenders based on specific criteria. This reduces guesswork and increases the likelihood of approval.

Submission and documentation can also be streamlined through automation. Standardized templates for executive summaries, financial analyses, and documentation packages ensure consistency and professionalism. Automation tools can organize and track required documents, reducing delays and improving efficiency. This allows you to handle multiple deals simultaneously without becoming overwhelmed.

Communication is another critical component of scalable systems. Automated follow-ups, status updates, and notifications keep all parties informed and engaged. This includes borrowers, lenders, and internal team members. Effective communication systems reduce bottlenecks and ensure that deals move forward smoothly. Artificial intelligence plays an increasingly important role in advanced structuring systems. AI can analyze large volumes of data, identify patterns, and provide insights that would be difficult to obtain manually. For example, AI can evaluate historical deal performance, predict approval likelihood, and suggest optimal structuring strategies. It can also assist in generating reports, summaries, and even marketing content.

Another key aspect of automation is workflow management. Advanced systems use project management tools to track the progress of each deal, assign tasks, and ensure that deadlines are met. This creates visibility and accountability, allowing you to manage a larger volume of transactions effectively.

Data management is also essential. Maintaining accurate and organized data on deals, clients, and lenders allows for better decision-making and continuous improvement. Advanced systems use databases and analytics tools to track performance, identify trends, and refine strategies over time.

Scalability also requires delegation and team building. As volume increases, it becomes impossible to handle every aspect of each deal individually. Advanced systems involve defining roles, delegating tasks, and creating processes that allow team members to contribute effectively. Automation supports this by providing clear workflows and reducing manual tasks.

Another important concept is continuous optimization. Systems should not remain static—they should evolve based on performance and feedback. Advanced structuring involves regularly reviewing processes, identifying inefficiencies, and implementing improvements. This iterative approach ensures that the system becomes more effective over time.

Risk management is also enhanced through automation. By standardizing processes and using data-driven analysis, advanced systems reduce the likelihood of errors and improve consistency. This leads to more reliable outcomes and higher approval rates.

As you build your system, it is important to maintain a balance between automation and human expertise. While technology can handle many tasks, critical decisions still require judgment and experience. Advanced structuring involves using automation to support decision-making, not replace it.

Ultimately, the goal of automation and systems is to create leverage. By reducing the time and effort required for each deal, you can handle more transactions, increase revenue, and scale your business. This transforms SBA commercial mortgage lending from a transactional activity into a scalable enterprise.

As you implement these strategies, you will begin to see exponential growth in your ability to structure and close deals. What once required significant time and effort can be accomplished more efficiently, allowing you to focus on higher-level strategy and growth.

Real-Life Math Example: Scaling SBA Deal Structuring with Systems and Automation

To understand the impact of automation and systems, let's walk through a real-world example comparing manual deal processing with an automated, system-driven approach.

Scenario 1: Manual Process

Deals per month: 5 Average deal size: $1,500,000 Average commission: 2%

Revenue per deal:

$\$1{,}500{,}000 \times 0.02 = \$30{,}000$

Monthly revenue:

$\$30{,}000 \times 5 = \$150{,}000$

Time per deal: 20 hours Total monthly hours:

20 × 5 = 100 hours

Scenario 2: Automated System

Deals per month: 15 Average deal size: $1,500,000 Average commission: 2%

Revenue per deal:

$30,000

Monthly revenue:

$30,000 × 15 = $450,000

Time per deal: 8 hours (due to automation) Total monthly hours:

8 × 15 = 120 hours

Efficiency Comparison

Manual:

100 hours for $150,000 → $1,500/hour

Automated:

120 hours for $450,000 → $3,750/hour

Annual Impact

Manual system:

$150,000 × 12 = $1,800,000

Automated system:

$450,000 × 12 = $5,400,000

Increase:

$5,400,000 – $1,800,000 = $3,600,000

Additional Benefits

Faster deal processing Higher approval rates Improved consistency Better client experience

Long-Term Scaling

If the system continues to improve and volume increases to 20 deals per month:

$30,000 × 20 = $600,000 monthly

Annual:

$600,000 × 12 = $7,200,000

Final Outcome

By implementing automation and systems, the borrower or loan professional achieves:

3× increase in deal volume 3× increase in revenue More efficient use of time Scalable business model

Key Takeaway

This example demonstrates that automation is not just about saving time—it is about creating leverage. By building systems that support deal structuring, you can significantly increase your output, improve performance, and scale your business to new levels.

Mastering this approach allows you to move beyond individual transactions and build a true SBA lending enterprise.

Chapter 15

Becoming the Deal Architect—Mastery, Positioning, and Building a Dominant SBA Commercial Mortgage Brand

At the highest level of SBA commercial mortgage loan structuring, the final transformation is not technical—it is identity. You move from being someone who understands deals to someone who designs them, controls them, and attracts them. You become the deal architect. This chapter is about stepping into that role fully—combining all the knowledge, systems, and strategies from this series into a powerful personal and business positioning that allows you to dominate your niche, attract high-quality opportunities, and operate at an elite level.

Most people in the SBA lending space operate reactively. They wait for deals, respond to borrower needs, and attempt to solve problems as they arise. Deal architects operate differently. They proactively design deals, influence outcomes, and position themselves as the go-to expert for complex transactions. They are not just participants in the process—they are the ones guiding it. This shift in mindset is what separates average performers from industry leaders. The foundation of becoming a deal architect is mastery. Mastery means understanding not just what works, but why it works. It means being able to look at any deal—no matter how complex—and quickly identify the key variables, risks, and opportunities. It means having the confidence to restructure transactions, challenge assumptions, and create solutions that others cannot see. This level of mastery comes from experience, repetition, and continuous learning.

Positioning is the next critical component. In a competitive market, how you present yourself matters as much as what you know. Deal architects position themselves as specialists in solving complex problems. They build a reputation for handling deals that others cannot close. This attracts higher-quality clients, better opportunities, and stronger partnerships. Advanced positioning involves clearly communicating your expertise, showcasing your results, and consistently delivering value.

Branding plays a major role in this positioning. A strong brand communicates trust, expertise, and reliability. It differentiates you from competitors and makes you memorable. For SBA deal architects, branding is not just about logos or marketing materials—it is about the perception you create through your work, communication, and results. Every interaction with a client or lender contributes to your brand. Content creation is a powerful tool for building authority. By sharing knowledge, insights, and strategies, you position yourself as an expert in the field. This can include articles, videos, webinars, or courses. Advanced deal architects use content to educate their audience, demonstrate their expertise, and attract new opportunities. Over time, this creates a steady flow of inbound leads and strengthens your market position.

Networking and partnerships are also essential. Building relationships with real estate agents, business brokers, accountants, attorneys, and lenders creates a network of referrals and opportunities. Deal architects understand the value of these relationships and invest time in developing and maintaining them. Strong partnerships can significantly increase deal flow and improve outcomes.

Another key aspect of becoming a deal architect is control over the deal flow. Instead of relying solely on external sources, advanced professionals create their own opportunities. This may involve targeted marketing, direct outreach, or leveraging data to identify potential deals. By controlling the flow of opportunities, you can focus on higher-quality transactions and increase your success rate.

Negotiation skills are also critical. Deal architects are not just structuring deals—they are negotiating terms, influencing outcomes, and aligning interests. This includes negotiating purchase prices, seller financing terms, loan structures, and partnership agreements. Strong negotiation skills can significantly impact the profitability and success of a deal.

Another important concept is value creation. Deal architects focus on creating value at every stage of the process. This includes identifying opportunities for improvement, optimizing structures, and maximizing financial outcomes. By consistently adding value, you build trust and strengthen your reputation.

Scalability is the next level of mastery. As your deal volume increases, it becomes essential to build systems and teams that support growth. This includes delegating tasks, automating processes, and creating workflows that allow you to handle more deals without sacrificing quality. Advanced deal architects operate at a level where they can manage multiple transactions simultaneously while maintaining high standards.

Another critical factor is decision-making. At the highest level, you are constantly making decisions that impact deals, clients, and your business. Advanced deal architects develop the ability to make informed, confident decisions quickly. This comes from experience, data analysis, and a deep understanding of the market. Resilience is also important. Not every deal will succeed, and challenges are inevitable. Deal architects view setbacks as learning opportunities and continue to refine their approach. This mindset allows them to maintain momentum and achieve long-term success.

Financial discipline is another key component. As your income grows, it is important to manage it effectively. This includes reinvesting in your business, building reserves, and planning for long-term growth. Advanced deal architects treat their business as an asset and manage it accordingly.

Another important aspect is leadership. As you build a team and expand your operations, your role shifts from doing everything yourself to guiding and supporting others. Effective leadership involves setting clear expectations, providing direction, and creating an environment where your team can succeed.

Ultimately, becoming a deal architect is about control—control over your deals, your business, and your future. It is about creating a system that allows you to operate at a high level consistently and achieve your goals.

As you reach the end of this series, you have the knowledge, tools, and strategies needed to operate at the highest level of SBA commercial mortgage lending. The next step is to apply these concepts, refine your approach, and continue growing.

The opportunity in this space is significant. By positioning yourself as a deal architect, you can create a powerful and sustainable business that generates income, builds wealth, and provides long-term financial freedom.

Real-Life Math Example: Scaling Income and Wealth as a Deal Architect

To understand the financial impact of becoming a deal architect, let's walk through a real-world example of how structuring, positioning, and scaling can increase income and wealth over time.

Phase 1: Entry Level

Deals per month: 3 Average deal size: $1,200,000 Commission: 2%

Revenue per deal:

$1,200,000 × 0.02 = $24,000

Monthly income:

$24,000 × 3 = $72,000

Annual income:

$72,000 × 12 = $864,000

Phase 2: Intermediate Growth

Deals per month: 6 Average deal size: $1,500,000

Revenue per deal:

$1,500,000 × 0.02 = $30,000

Monthly income:

$30,000 × 6 = $180,000

Annual income:

$180,000 × 12 = $2,160,000

Phase 3: Advanced Deal Architect

Deals per month: 10 Average deal size: $2,000,000

Revenue per deal:

$2,000,000 × 0.02 = $40,000

Monthly income:

$40,000 × 10 = $400,000

Annual income:

$400,000 × 12 = $4,800,000

Adding Portfolio Income

Assume the deal architect also acquires properties generating $20,000 annual cash flow each.

After 5 acquisitions:

$20,000 × 5 = $100,000 annual passive income

After 10 acquisitions:

$20,000 × 10 = $200,000 annual passive income

Total Income at Advanced Level

Active income:

$4,800,000

Passive income:

$200,000

Total:

$5,000,000 annually

Long-Term Wealth Growth

Assume each property appreciates by $200,000 over time.

10 properties:

$200,000 × 10 = $2,000,000 in equity growth

Combined with loan paydown, total equity may exceed $4,000,000.

Final Outcome

By becoming a deal architect, the individual achieves:

Multi-million dollar annual income Diversified income streams Significant equity growth Scalable business model

Key Takeaway

This example demonstrates that mastering SBA deal structuring is not just about closing loans—it is about building a business and creating long-term wealth. By scaling deal volume, increasing deal size, and investing in assets, you can achieve exponential growth.

The ultimate goal is not just success, but dominance in your niche. By applying the principles in this chapter, you can position yourself as a leader in SBA commercial mortgage lending and create a powerful, sustainable future.

Closing Thoughts

From Knowledge to Execution—Building Your SBA Commercial Mortgage Legacy

As you reach the end of this journey through advanced SBA commercial mortgage loan structuring, it is important to recognize that what you now possess is far more than knowledge. You have developed a framework, a mindset, and a strategic approach that has the potential to transform not only how you approach deals, but how you build your entire financial future. The difference between those who succeed at a high level and those who remain average is not access to information—it is execution. This final section is about turning everything you have learned into consistent, focused action.

Throughout this series, you have seen how deals can be reshaped, optimized, and transformed through structuring. You have learned how to analyze cash flow, design capital stacks, align ownership structures, select lenders strategically, and position deals for approval. More importantly, you have learned how to think differently. Instead of seeing obstacles, you now see variables. Instead of seeing declines, you see opportunities for restructuring. This shift in perspective is what allows you to operate at a higher level. The SBA lending space offers one of the most powerful opportunities available in business and real estate. It allows you to control large assets with relatively small amounts of capital, leverage government-backed programs to reduce risk, and create long-term wealth through cash flow and appreciation. However, these opportunities are not automatic. They must be identified, structured, and executed with precision. This is where your expertise becomes your greatest asset.

One of the most important lessons to carry forward is that every deal is unique. While there are common principles and strategies, no two transactions are exactly the same. This means that your ability to adapt, analyze, and innovate will be critical. The best deal architects are not those who follow a rigid formula, but those who understand the underlying principles and apply them creatively to each situation.

Another key takeaway is the importance of consistency. Success in SBA lending is not built on one or two deals—it is built on a series of well-structured transactions over time. Each deal you complete adds to your experience, strengthens your reputation, and expands your network. This cumulative effect is what allows you to scale your efforts and achieve long-term success.

Relationships will play a central role in your journey. Whether it is with borrowers, lenders, partners, or referral sources, the connections you build will influence your opportunities and outcomes. Trust and credibility are earned through consistent performance and professionalism. By delivering value and maintaining strong relationships, you position yourself for continued growth.

Another important aspect is continuous learning. The SBA landscape, market conditions, and lending practices are constantly evolving. Staying informed and adaptable will ensure that you remain competitive and effective. This may involve keeping up with industry trends, refining your strategies, or exploring new opportunities. The willingness to learn and grow is a defining characteristic of top performers.

As you move forward, it is also important to maintain a long-term perspective. While individual deals are important, they should be viewed as part of a larger strategy. This includes building a portfolio, creating multiple income streams, and positioning yourself for financial independence. Advanced structuring is not just about closing deals—it is about creating a sustainable system that supports your goals.

Risk management should always remain a priority. While the opportunities in SBA lending are significant, they come with inherent risks. By maintaining discipline, preserving liquidity, and making informed decisions, you can manage these risks effectively. A balanced approach ensures that growth is sustainable and that setbacks are minimized.

Execution is where everything comes together. It is the bridge between knowledge and results. Taking action, making decisions, and following through on opportunities is what ultimately determines your success. This requires confidence, discipline, and a willingness to step outside of your comfort zone. Each deal you pursue is an opportunity to apply what you have learned and refine your approach.

Another critical element is focus. With so many opportunities available, it is easy to become distracted or overwhelmed. By focusing on high-quality deals and aligning your efforts with your goals, you can maximize your impact and efficiency. This strategic focus allows you to achieve better results with less wasted effort.

The concept of leverage extends beyond financing—it applies to your time, resources, and efforts. By building systems, automating processes, and leveraging relationships, you can increase your output and scale your business. This allows you to handle more deals, generate more income, and create greater impact without proportionally increasing your workload.

As you continue to grow, your role will evolve. You may start as a borrower or loan professional, but over time, you can become an investor, a strategist, and a leader. This progression opens up new opportunities and expands your influence. Embracing this evolution will allow you to operate at a higher level and achieve greater success.

Another important consideration is your impact on others. By helping borrowers secure financing, supporting businesses, and contributing to economic growth, you play a role in creating opportunities for others. This broader impact adds meaning to your work and reinforces the value of what you do.

The journey ahead will not always be easy. There will be challenges, setbacks, and moments of uncertainty. However, these experiences are part of the process and provide valuable lessons. By maintaining a resilient mindset and staying committed to your goals, you can overcome obstacles and continue moving forward.

It is also important to celebrate your progress. Each deal you close, each challenge you overcome, and each milestone you achieve is a step toward your larger vision. Recognizing these achievements helps maintain motivation and reinforces your commitment to success.

As you look to the future, consider what you want to build.

Whether it is a portfolio of properties, a successful lending business, or a broader financial empire, your vision will guide your actions. By aligning your efforts with this vision, you create a clear path forward.

The principles and strategies outlined in this series provide a strong foundation, but your success will ultimately depend on how you apply them. Taking action, learning from experience, and continuously refining your approach will allow you to achieve your goals and create lasting success.

In closing, remember that the true value of this knowledge lies in its application. You now have the tools to structure deals, solve problems, and create opportunities. The next step is to use them. By doing so, you can transform not only your business but your financial future.

The opportunity is in front of you. The knowledge is in your hands. The only thing left is to take action and build the legacy you envision.

How to Get a Personalized SBA Commercial Mortgage Review

If you found this book helpful, you may want to see how these strategies apply to your specific financial situation.

SBA commercial mortgage financing is highly customized—your business income, financial statements, credit profile, property type, industry, and long-term goals all play a role in determining what you qualify for and how your loan should be structured.

Every borrower's situation is different. Your revenue trends, business model, tax returns, debt obligations, ownership structure, and the type of commercial property you are purchasing, refinancing, or building all impact your options. The strategies and examples in this book are designed to teach you how SBA commercial mortgage loans work—but your actual loan approval, terms, and structure can only be determined by analyzing your real financial profile.

If you would like a no-obligation SBA Commercial Mortgage review, you can request one here:

Email: info@FinibiMortgage.com

A licensed mortgage broker will review your business financials, income structure, credit profile, and goals, and explain what SBA financing options may be available to you—including:

• SBA 7(a) commercial mortgage loans• SBA 504 fixed-rate commercial real estate financing• Owner-occupied property qualification strategies• Business acquisition with real estate financing• Commercial refinance and cash-out strategies• Construction and expansion loan structuring• Advanced SBA deal structuring to maximize approval

No cost. No pressure. No obligation.

Sincerely,

Joseph G. Correa

Finibi Mortgage Inc.

Licensed Mortgage Broker

About the Author

Joseph G. Correa is a licensed mortgage broker and the founder of Finibi Mortgage, a Florida-based brokerage specializing in SBA commercial mortgage loans, non-QM lending, and strategic real estate financing solutions for business owners, entrepreneurs, and investors.

With more than two decades of experience in mortgage lending, underwriting, and deal structuring, Joseph has helped thousands of clients secure financing for commercial real estate, business acquisitions, and complex transactions using both traditional and alternative lending strategies.

Unlike traditional loan officers who focus only on basic qualification, Joseph's approach emphasizes **cash flow analysis, deal structuring, and strategic financing**. He believes that business owners should not be limited by rigid lending formulas, but instead empowered by understanding how to structure deals that align with lender guidelines and maximize approval potential.

Joseph is widely recognized for his expertise in:

• SBA 7(a) and SBA 504 commercial mortgage loans• Owner-occupied commercial real estate financing• Business acquisition with real estate structuring• Commercial refinance and cash flow optimization• Construction and expansion financing• Advanced loan structuring and approval strategy

Through his education platform, Finibi Academy, Joseph has trained tens of thousands of students worldwide in mortgage strategy, real estate investing, credit optimization, and financial independence.

He created the *SBA Commercial Mortgage Loan Mastery Series* to provide a clear, step-by-step roadmap for borrowers and professionals who want to understand, qualify for, and scale commercial real estate using SBA financing.

His mission is simple:

To help business owners use strategic financing to acquire assets, build cash flow, and create long-term wealth.

When he is not structuring loans or writing, Joseph works with clients across the United States to design customized SBA financing strategies aligned with their business goals and growth plans.

The SBA Commercial Mortgage Loan Mastery Series Roadmap

The Complete Guide to Using SBA Financing to Build Commercial Real Estate and Business Wealth

The purpose of *The SBA Commercial Mortgage Loan Mastery Series* is to give business owners, investors, and mortgage professionals the exact strategies used by lenders and underwriters—translated into simple, practical steps you can apply in real life.

This series takes you from beginner to advanced mastery of how to qualify, structure, and scale commercial real estate and business financing using SBA mortgage loans.

Each book builds on the last. You are not just learning how to get approved—you are learning how to control your approvals and scale your opportunities.

Book 1 — SBA Commercial Mortgage Loan Fundamentals Understand how SBA mortgage programs work, including 7(a) and 504 loans, and how to qualify.

Book 2 — Getting Approved for an SBA Commercial Mortgage Loan Learn step-by-step strategies to meet lender requirements and secure funding.

Book 3 — Owner-Occupied Property Financing with SBA Loans Learn how to buy or refinance your business property using SBA financing.

Book 4 — Buying a Business and Real Estate with SBA Financing Acquire a business and its property in one structured transaction.

Book 5 — SBA 7(a) Mortgage Loan Strategies Master flexible loan structures for business and real estate funding.

Book 6 — SBA 504 Mortgage Loans for Commercial Real Estate Use long-term fixed-rate financing for large property acquisitions.

Book 7 — Refinancing Commercial Debt with SBA Loans Lower payments, improve cash flow, and restructure existing debt.

Book 8 — SBA Loans for Construction and Expansion Build, renovate, and scale commercial properties with structured financing.

Book 9 — SBA Loan Requirements, Rates, and Structures Understand how to compare options and choose the best loan.

Book 10 — Advanced SBA Commercial Mortgage Structuring Engineer approvals and maximize leverage using expert strategies.

This series is designed to move you from:

Understanding → Execution → Scaling → Mastery

By the end, you will not just know how to qualify—you will know how to structure, analyze, and scale deals like a professional.

Educational & Financial Disclaimer

The *SBA Commercial Mortgage Loan Mastery Series* is intended for educational and informational purposes only.

This content is designed to help readers understand SBA commercial mortgage lending, real estate financing strategies, and business acquisition concepts. It is not financial, legal, tax, or investment advice.

Joseph G. Correa and Live Stronger Faster are not acting as your personal financial advisor, attorney, accountant, or mortgage professional through this publication.

SBA loan programs, underwriting guidelines, interest rates, and lender requirements may change at any time and vary by lender.

All examples in this series are for illustration purposes only and do not guarantee approval or results.

Always consult with licensed professionals before making financial decisions.

Risk Disclosure

SBA commercial mortgage lending and real estate investing involve risk.

Business performance, income stability, interest rate changes, market conditions, and lender guidelines can all impact loan approval and financial outcomes.

Borrowing against real estate or using leverage increases both potential returns and risk.

Failure to repay a loan may result in foreclosure and loss of property.

Cash flow, rental income, appreciation, and business performance are not guaranteed.

All strategies presented in this series are educational and must be evaluated based on your individual financial situation.

You are solely responsible for your financial decisions.

www.ingramcontent.com/pod-product-compliance
Ingram Content Group UK Ltd.
Pitfield, Milton Keynes, MK11 3LW, UK
UKHW020159290926
15471UKWH00005B/965

9 798295 820687